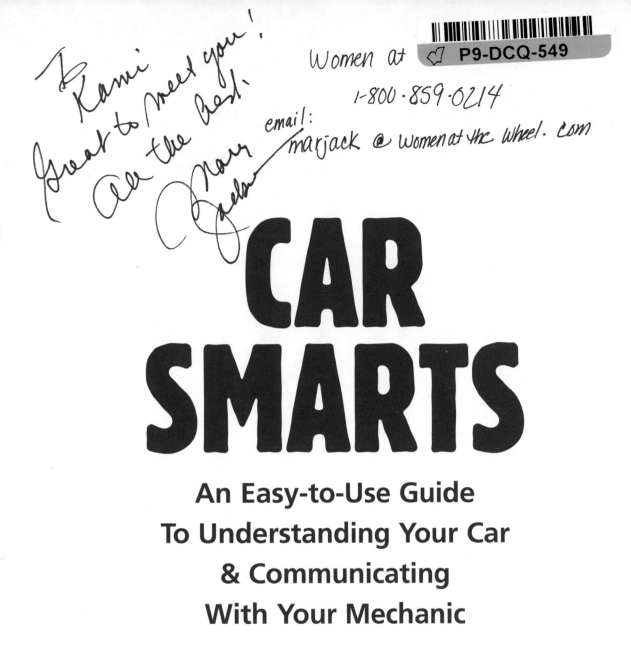

Women at
1-800·859·0214
email: marjack @ Women at the Wheel. com

To Rami
Great to meet you!
All the Best.
Mary
Jackson

CAR SMARTS

An Easy-to-Use Guide
To Understanding Your Car
& Communicating
With Your Mechanic

Mary Jackson

John Muir Publications
Santa Fe, New Mexico

John Muir Publications, P.O. Box 613, Santa Fe, New Mexico 87504

Printed in the United States of America
First printing October 1998

Library of Congress Cataloging-in-Publication Data

Jackson, Mary, 1946–
        Car Smarts : an easy-to-use guide to understanding your car and communicating with
your mechanic / Mary Jackson. — 3rd ed.
                p. cm.
        Rev. ed. of: The greaseless guide to car care. 2nd ed. 1995.
        Includes index.
        ISBN: 1-56261-457-6
        1. Automobile—Maintenance and repair—Popular works.
2. Automobiles—Design and construction—Popular works.
I. Jackson, Mary, 1946– Greaseless guide to car care. II. Title.
TL152.J275 1998
629.28'72—dc21   98-34950
                                                                    CIP

Editor: Julie Lefevre, Dianna Delling
Production: Marie J.T. Vigil
Cover design: Rebecca Cook
Illustrations: Maria Voris and William Rotsaert
Printing: Publishers Press

Distributed to the book trade by
Publishers Group West
Berkeley, California

Contents

Preface

"Garage-ese" is a language developed and spoken by motor-heads to other motor-heads. Unfortunately, it is also spoken to non-motor-heads. This book has been written and revised to close the communication gap between the two. It is exclusively for those who may never tune or troubleshoot but who, nevertheless, would like to be able to speak confidently, to understand, and to be clearly understood when it comes to buying a car or having a car repaired, and further, who would like to avoid unnecessary repairs and overcharges while getting the longest serviceable life out of their automobile.

As the only girl growing up in a family of five boys, I did not learn garage-ese at home. Information about cars was placed on a "need to know" basis, and in our family, girls did not need to know.

That worked fine until I began driving my own car. I quickly discovered that I had a definite need to know. I had a need to know about new sounds coming from my car. Did they mean a $2 or a $200 repair? Or should I begin looking for a new car? I had a need to know about routine maintenance. Was I doing the right thing by having the engine oil changed every leap year? I had a need to know about repairs and pricing. Was I being treated fairly, or did service providers identify my obvious ignorance as fair game? Having almost no knowledge of my car and no language with which to learn about it, I struggled hopelessly with repair explanations and in the end, reluctantly and blindly delegated full responsibility to mechanics. My vulnerability, frustration, and sense of powerlessness ended when I moved to a small Vermont town and, in an effort to avoid starvation, took a job in a local body shop.

There, among the tack rags and paint fumes, while doing general repair work, I had my first opportunity to look inside cars. Engines, transmissions, and brakes began to make sense as I peeled back the outside and observed their basic parts and relationships, all the while, like a three-year-old, asking hundreds of "why" questions.

This book is intended to pass on my learning experience, sans paint fumes, with the hope that knowing the basics about cars will help you make Car-Smart decisions. This book is not an exhaustive work, but rather a framework for building car care confidence and providing protection from car repair rip-off.

I would like to thank Dan Donza for opening up the world of cars to me and for helping me in too many ways to mention to make this book possible; and Lenny Bisceglia for his knowledge, time, patience, and unique explanations of how cars tick; and to the many other technicians who contributed in some way to my assembling this information. Thanks also go to the participants who have attended my workshops. Their humor, intelligent questions, and insightful comments have been an invaluable help.

I am very fortunate to have as my publisher John Muir Publications. And Maria Voris' and William Rotsaert's illustrations have made the words come alive as I had always hoped they would, with clarity and humor.

Speaking of words, I owe much to Ray Fry, a true car guy, who patiently helped me find the right ones. His love and knowledge of automobiles is an inspiration, and I am grateful for the time and effort he devoted to this edition.

I want to thank my brothers, Danny, Lenny, Mike, Kevin, and Mark, for being the very funny men they are, and for teaching me the invaluable place of humor in my life and work. There is also my other family, the Marshalls, whose love and encouragement continue to make a huge difference. A special thank-you goes to my husband and friend, Jim Marshall, who contributed in every imaginable way to helping me write this book, but especially for convincing me that I could.

And finally there are my parents, the late Leonard and Pat Horan, who taught me to enjoy life and to choose a job I would love, that any limits I would encounter in my life would be self-imposed, and that there is no knowledge that is either inappropriate or unattainable.

1
INTRODUCTION

Cars and trucks play an integral part in our lives. They may well be the objects of lust for some, but most of us simply depend on that car or truck to get us from point A to point B.

Whether the car is purchased or leased, new or used, we all end up investing a large part of our paychecks in the care and nurturing of our "wheels." The process of buying and maintaining a car can be overwhelming. Pricing, finance rates, model variations, vehicle sizes, standard equipment, stand-alone options versus packages, warranties, consumer group ratings, safety pros and cons, not to mention the size of your pocketbook—all have a bearing on what you choose in the end. Maintenance and repair can be confusing and costly. But dealing with automobiles, especially for those who claim to be nontechnical (hey, that's the majority of us), doesn't have to be a frustrating and expensive experience.

Your Car-Smart decisions will translate into spending less and getting more.

Knowledge of "garage-ese" has become increasingly important in communicating about our cars to service providers.

The key is to be faithful: faithful to your owner's manual, faithful to one good service provider with an efficient and decent staff, and dedicated to learning more about how your car or truck really works.

That is what this book is all about: making you more knowledgeable, eliminating hassles, saving money. Sound good so far?

I'll venture a guess that your mom or dad never took you by the hand to show you the secrets of the V-8 versus the slant six. I'll wager further that you didn't get together with your pals to give the ole Chevy or Toyota a tune up unless you grew up in a family where some member was a backyard mechanic. Without an automotive foundation or framework of understanding, what goes on under the hood of your car may be as mysterious as the transporter on the starship *Enterprise*.

In my own experience as a kid, whenever there was a problem with a car, my five brothers, Danny, Lenny, Mike, Kevin, and Mark, would run out to the car, lift the hood, and begin discussing the virtues of carburetors, spark plugs, and distributors. The message I heard, while I watched from a distance, was that girls did not need to know about cars. Excellent, I thought, one less thing for me to worry about. And it was excellent—until I was out on my own and got my first car, a beat-up old VW Bug.

I hated dealing with auto mechanics. They seemed to

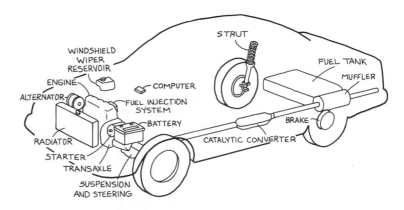

Cars are complex, yes, but also systematic and, with a little study, understandable. This car has a typical front-wheel-drive layout.

speak a foreign language that I called "garage-ese." "EGRS," "PCVS," "rotors," and "calipers" were just a few of the technical terms that were rattled at me in rapid succession. Being auto illiterate, I frequently suspected that I was buying unnecessary repairs at inflated prices.

Things changed for the better right after college. I moved to a ski resort in upstate Vermont to indulge my passion for skiing. I took a job in a local auto body shop while pursuing a master's degree in political science. With on-the-job training, I spent the next 13 years painting, sanding, and welding. I discovered that the secrets of cars were far more interesting than those of the Pentagon. I also found another passion: automobiles.

Among the paint fumes and twisted metal, I learned that my five brothers knew less about cars than any other five human beings on earth. More important, I realized there was no mystery. Automobiles, I discovered, were logical, systematic, and understandable. As with any system, if you began with the basics and used a layperson's language, cars could be broken down and understood.

I discovered that engine oil works like the blood in our bodies: It cools and cleans, it is pumped by a pump similar to the heart, and over time it fills with a cholesterol-like substance called sludge. Knowing that, I began to have my engine oil changed frequently. With other preventive maintenance measures, my car became more reliable, lasted longer, and cost me less.

Over the years, many female friends and acquaintances came to me to get advice about car problems and purchases. Many reported that in dealing with their cars, they had been taken advantage of because they were women.

In 1983 I borrowed a local mechanic's garage after hours and invited a handful of women friends over for some car-care pointers and a peek under the hood. Although I didn't know it at the time, I was presenting the first Women at the Wheel® car-care clinic. My life was about to change in a way that I had never imagined. I had discovered a third passion: a love for educating and entertaining in the same breath.

A basic understanding of how cars work can help you avoid unnecessary or overpriced repairs.

Before I was autoliterate, when I heard a strange ka-thunk coming from under the hood, I did what many others do when they hear a strange ka-thunk: I turned up the radio.

The program was an instant success, and soon I was lecturing full time on the joys of demystifying automobiles. From San Diego to Bangor, from Miami to Seattle, women (and men) turned out in force to learn about automobiles in nontechnical language. I began every workshop with the following explanation:

Cars and Bicycles

A car works something like a bicycle. When the cyclist pedals, she or he generates up-and-down power through the legs. That power makes both the bicycle chain and the wheels turn. Up-and-down power is converted into rotational power. And down the road the bicycle goes.

Inside each car's engine there are three or more round metal plugs called **pistons**. These are attached to a metal bar called the **crankshaft**. Like the cyclist's legs, these pistons move up and down. Their up-and-down motion makes the crankshaft turn, which, through the **transmission**, turns the car's wheels. Once again, up-and-down power is converted into rotational power, and down the road your car goes.

Just as the cyclist needs a balanced diet to perform well, so does your car's engine. Instead of vegetables and protein, a car wants air and gasoline (or an alternate source of fuel).

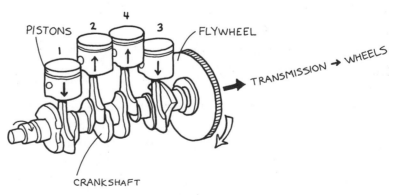

A car works something like a bicycle. In both, up-and-down power is converted into rotational power.

Your car's engine needs a balanced diet of air and fuel to generate power, just as the bicyclist requires food.

❖

Compressing air and gasoline inside an engine and adding a hot spark is like dropping a match into a container of gasoline. Boom! The resulting expanding gases push the pistons down hard. Because the explosions happen over the tops of the pistons at slightly different moments, they move rapidly up and down at different times. This movement causes the crankshaft to spin and the wheels to turn.

If the cyclist's diet is unbalanced, he or she won't have the get-up-and-go to generate power. Hills that were once a piece of cake now look like Pikes Peak. Cars also suffer if their diet is unbalanced. Too much air, too much fuel, or a spark that is delivered at the wrong time can result in poor performance. Hard starting, stalling, surging, and low gas mileage are all symptoms that may be related to an unbalanced diet.

The Proper Care and Feeding of Your Car

Just as you routinely visit your dentist to have your teeth cared for, check ups and adjustments are vital to your car's health. It takes a trained mechanic to perform the preventive maintenance that will keep your car running

Air + fuel + fire = power

As the air/fuel mixture explodes and expands, it pushes the pistons down, causing the crankshaft to spin and the wheels to turn.

❖

smoothly with a minimal amount of repairs. Preventive maintenance also fights two enemies that arouse dread in the heart of every car: dirt and friction.

Dirt can block the flow of vital fluids in the car. It can also act as an irritant between the engine's tight-fitting, moving metal parts. Like a piece of sand in an oyster shell, dirt scratches the smooth surfaces of the engine's internal parts, causing them to wear prematurely. Unlike sand in the oyster, you won't get a pearl—but you can count on a gem of a repair bill.

Friction, the abrasive action of two objects rubbing against each other, results in heat and wear. The deadly duo of dirt and friction can send your car to an early grave, after a lifetime of expensive repairs, if preventive maintenance is not performed on time.

The appropriate maintenance schedule for your car is found in your owner's manual. There you will find two service categories, normal and severe service. Most of our cars will need the severe service category, since most of us do a lot of stop-and-go driving.

By being faithful to your owner's manual and service schedule, you will spend a limited amount of money every year to avoid the expensive replacement of prematurely worn parts. In addition, a well-maintained engine starts more reliably, uses less fuel, and pollutes the planet less.

Granted, it's no page-turner, but your owner's manual contains essential information about the proper care and feeding of your vehicle.

Most of you probably have your owner's manual sitting by the bedside table, within easy reach, so that you can go over and over those particularly fun-filled pages. You know, the dog-eared ones? No? You haven't read it? You took it out of the glove box once to find out how the defroster worked in a blinding snowstorm?

Hey, would you do that with a new camera? Owner's manuals may seem dull, but they contain extremely important information about your car, including the specific grade of oil and gasoline that you should use.

No owner's manual? Contact the parts department of a car dealership that sells your type of vehicle and ask them to order one for you. Expect to pay a small amount.

So put down that best-seller and add a brand new dimension to your reading. And when you're done, put your manual in the glove compartment where it will be handy. Together with this book, the manual holds a vital key to a long and healthy life for your automobile.

Cars suffer if their diet is unbalanced.

Car Smarts

Over the years, I have given hundreds of seminars intended to demystify automobiles and have talked to tens of thousands of people. Through Women at the Wheel®, I have given car-care clinics, written newspaper articles, and appeared on radio and television shows. More information is available on my Web site: www.womenatthewheel.com. I stay informed about important automotive developments by speaking frequently at industry conferences and events and attending international auto shows.

I believe gender can be a factor in getting a fair deal from auto dealers and repair people, but it doesn't have to be. Whether your label is Ms., Miss, Mrs., or Mr., this book can help you to level the playing field.

A lot of things have changed since the last edition of this book. Most new cars and trucks are better built, smarter, cleaner, and safer. But they still work on the same principles, and there is much you can do to protect your car and your pocketbook. Specifically, this book will help you:

➤ Negotiate the best price or lease on a new or used car or truck

➤ Understand what your warranty really covers

➤ Keep informed on the latest safety and technology information

➤ Discover what makes your car or truck tick, and why it quits ticking

➤ Find an honest and competent auto professional

➤ Understand your salesperson and mechanic

➤ Extend the life of your car or truck

➤ Protect yourself from unneeded, phony, or overpriced maintenance and repairs

➤ Make eloquent automotive small talk at cocktail parties

You can use this book in several different ways. Each chapter explains a major automotive system and how it works, explains how you can make these systems last longer, gives you money-saving tips, helps you troubleshoot common problems, and gives you a sense of the severity of others.

You can learn a little or you can learn a lot. If you want to know how your automatic transmission works in depth, the information is here. If you want just the bare facts—a few pointers on how to talk to mechanics when that transmission starts to shift lazily—you can find that here too.

Armed with the information in this book, you can learn your car's logical secrets. Then, your Car-Smart decisions will translate into spending less and getting more. Ultimately, I hope this book will help make all your journeys smooth.

2
BUYING AND LEASING

Buying a new or used car or truck is probably the second biggest investment you're likely to make. These days there is an embarrassment of riches to choose from—so many choices that choosing can turn into a chore. This chapter suggests where and when to buy or lease a new or used vehicle, how to negotiate like a street merchant, how to conduct a test drive, and what the warranty covers. It defines in easy-to-understand language the different vehicles types, engines, drivetrain alternatives, and options. It will help you get the vehicle you want at a price that fits you and your budget.

More and more, car buyers are turning to the Internet for online shopping.

There are, of course, a variety of methods you can use to approach the buying decision: 1) kick tires, slam doors, nod sagely as the salesperson discusses torque and power-to-weight ratios, 2) stuff your mouth with cotton, grab the salesperson by the throat, and say you've got an offer that he or she can't refuse, 3) arm yourself with realistic facts and figures. If you choose the third option, you're more likely to drive a hard bargain and end up with the new or used vehicle that's right for you and your budget. It's really a matter of following a few simple rules.

Do Your Homework

Smart buying begins at home, long before you enter the dealership showroom or go online. When you arrive knowing what you want in a car or truck, and how much you can afford, you reduce the chances of ending up in a vehicle you don't want at a price you really can't afford.

Based on your income and expenses, determine how much you can afford to spend on a monthly payment, including taxes, registration fees, maintenance, gas, and tires. Call your insurance agent to find out if a new vehicle carries a higher insurance rate. It often does. You may love that flashy red sports car, but you may not like the hefty insurance premium that goes with it. The last thing you want is to buy a car you love and not be able to afford the care it needs to go the distance—or not be able to live the life you want because you're in hock up to your neck.

Ask Yourself Before You Shop

➤ Is your car a way of making a statement to the world or simply a way to get from point A to point B?

➤ How do you primarily use your car? Commuting back and forth to work? Chauffeuring clients, kids, or pets? Long trips? Hauling groceries or cargo? Getting away from the madding crowd? If you carry adult passengers frequently, you'll want to check both front and rear seat headroom and legroom.

➤ How much trunk or cargo space do you need? Enough for your briefcase and golf clubs? Enough for bags and bags of groceries? Will your vehicle be a "toy box" filled with Windsurfers, mountain bikes, and kayaks?

➤ How many miles do you drive a year?

➤ Where do you typically drive: city streets, highways, back roads, steep hills?

➤ What is the weather like where you live? Do you drive on snow-covered or icy roads?

➤ Will this vehicle be garaged? If so, is garage space tight? You'll want to know the vehicle's length, width, and height.

➤ How long do you intend to keep this vehicle?

➤ Do you see significant career or family changes in the near future?

Buying Safety: Understanding Vehicle Safety Ratings

Safety is, and should be, a primary concern with consumers today. More and more product safety information is being released by manufacturers—to their credit—and independent agencies. You will certainly want to investigate the crash tests and ratings of any vehicle that you are considering.

The National Highway Traffic and Safety Administration (www.nhtsa.gov) lists frontal crash ratings based on fixed-barrier, 35-mile-per-hour frontal collisions for passenger vehicles. The higher the number of stars—up to five—the better.

The Insurance Institute for Highway Safety (IIHS)

With as many types of vehicles on the market today as there are flavors of ice cream, the task of choosing the right one can seem daunting. It doesn't have to be.

Glossary of Vehicle Types

Convertibles
Who doesn't yearn for the rush of the wind in their hair, the hot sun beating down, and a sky as blue as the ocean? Even with a small cargo area, a dwarfish rear seat, and diminished safety and security, convertibles are still the most fun on the block.

Coupes
Sedans less the two rear doors, coupes are returning with gusto to the sub-compact and compact market. Their appeal has always been about style: they look like they're moving while they're standing still. Caution! Hauling children and car seats out of the rear compartment imitates a circus act.

Hatchbacks
They come in sedan or coupe form, although it's difficult to find one beyond the smallest of vehicles. They are convenient by design: the entire back end opens up to reveal a large open cargo space. Their drawbacks include the lack of privacy for cargo and Fido's bad humor after trips on those thin, folding rear seats.

Minivans
They carry a ton of passengers and luggage and provide easy access for all. They come with three or four side doors—sliding or swing out. They have bucket or bench seats that fold up or pop out, in cloth or leather. They have a higher center of gravity than sedans. Hence they give a great view of the road (unless you're following one). The price for that height is some sacrifice of performance and handling.

Pickup Trucks
The good the bad and the ugly? Hardly. Today's pickup trucks, with their car-like interiors, stylish cabs, and rakish plastic-lined open boxes or beds can hold their own at a debutante's ball. The debutante is probably driving one anyway! Originally designed for a limited number of passengers and with two doors, pickups have been adding both lately. They are available in many sizes and with a wide assortment of powertrains, options, and towing and hauling capacities.

Sedans
The most popular vehicles, sedans are four-door passenger cars with a separate trunk, sometimes connected to the interior via a folding rear seat. They

come in every size and price range; with four-, six, or eight-cylinder engines and with front-, rear-, or all-wheel drive. While sedans are often thought of as conservative, don't overlook "sport packages" that can turn driving to the corner store into a treat.

Sport Utility Vehicles

"SUVs" are often built on truck frames with carlike interiors. They offer superior visibility and impressive cargo capacity. Ask them to go off-road and they can be as adventurous as they are irresistible. But many are gas-guzzlers and devilish to get in and out of. New smaller versions, "UTEs" (short for *utility*), are more urban and compact, and less expensive, than their larger siblings.

Sports Cars

These two-seater coupes or convertibles are designed primarily for performance and handling. Blood flows in the veins of real men and real women when they hear the growl of a sports car. Usually rear-wheel drive and powerful, sports cars ride low to the ground and represent the ultimate driver's experience. Comfort and convenience might take a back seat—but there isn't any back seat!

Station Wagons

They look and handle much like sedans because that's what they are—sedans with an additional compartment in back. These casual workhorses carry everything from golf clubs to Grandma to gravel and never complain. Once almost extinct because of the rise in popularity of the minivan, station wagons are back in a variety of sizes and prices. Their drawbacks include the lack of privacy for cargo.

What type of vehicle is right for you?

performs very different tests on selected vehicles, usually 40-mile-per-hour "offset collisions" with two vehicles of equal size and weight. The ratings—good, acceptable, marginal, and poor—can be viewed on the Institute's Web site: www.highwaysafety.com.

It's important to keep in mind when reviewing this information that a subcompact that is rated "good" may not be as safe as a large sedan with the same rating. It's also important to learn about recent safety improvements in the vehicles you are considering. For more about new safety systems and improvements, see Chapter 16.

Options

Times were, if you wanted a red base-model car (the lowest-priced version of that model) with a beige interior and optional air-conditioning, the factory would custom build the car for you. You anxiously waited up to four months, but eventually the car arrived—just the way you wanted it and just as the cold weather set in.

Today that red base-model car comes only with a gray interior. To get air-conditioning, you are required to also pay for four-speed automatic transmission, outside mirrors, and electric door locks. Together, these items make up an "option package." If you continue to insist on that beige interior, you'll have to buy a more expensive trim level that also features fold-down seats.

Today's way of doing business may seem at first confusing, but a factory Web site, a good brochure, and time taken to digest the information will help you understand your choice of models and their standard features, plus upgraded model choices. The key is to purchase only those options that you really want, that represent good value, or that will add resale value to the vehicle.

Make a wish list of what you must have and what you'd like to have. What does your current car lack, if anything? Some options just glitter, but others really make driving easier, safer, and more comfortable. Among these are power steering, power brakes, power

Don't be talked into options you don't need.

door locks, power windows, air-conditioning, and ABS brakes.

Other options—rustproofing, paint protection (an overpriced wax job), fabric protection (do it yourself for much less)—are unnecessary and, in some cases, can void your warranty. Call your manufacturer's 800 customer-service number if you have a question about any option that isn't factory-installed.

Do not assume that because the dealer doesn't have a vehicle with the specific options you want that no one does. Ask about a "dealer trade": all dealers have relationships with other dealers, and if they want to make the effort for your business, they may be able to trade their "in-stock" vehicle for the exact one you want.

The Story on Color

Look out, white and shades of greens. You've been the overall color choice in recent years, but here come the beiges, golds, and champagnes, the rust and earth tones. Ultimately, the car's color must please you, but remember you're probably going to have to live with that color for a long time.

Ask yourself: does your vehicle sit outside in the elements, especially in the blazing sun? (Black draws heat and red often fades.) Do you wash and polish your vehicle regularly? If the answer is no, you may be better off with low-maintenance white.

Shopping Around

Gather brochures from local dealerships. While you're there, pay careful attention to the way the staff treats you. Are they helpful, responsive, and respectful? If not, you'll know where not to buy.

Much of your research can be done inexpensively, at your local library or bookstore. Read *Consumer Reports* auto issue. Check out a vehicle's repair history, a good indicator of reliability. If any of the vehicles you're considering is a brand-new model, it will not have a repair history. Consider other models that do, or wait a year and see what develops with the new model.

Read reviews in some of the popular car-buff magazines including *Automobile, Car and Driver, Motor Trend, Road and Track,* and *AutoWeek.* Their road test reports and articles are filled with invaluable information that can help you choose wisely. But keep in mind that their reporters are real car buffs. They worship power, performance, and handling. Their priorities and yours might not be the same.

After you've done your homework on models, it's wise to investigate the reputation of the dealership, broker, or online service you're considering.

Where to Buy

You can shop for new vehicles by visiting a dealership, hiring a buyer broker, or going to an online service. Online sites vary in features and usefulness. Some offer 3-D views of vehicle exteriors and interiors. You'll also find vehicle specifications, including option packages, warranties, and, in some cases, estimated maintenance and repair costs (see the list of online services on page 17).

Even if you buy through a broker or online, you will want to visit a dealership to test-drive the vehicle you have chosen. You will also need to work with a dealership about any problems that come up while the vehicle is still under warranty. Take a tour of the dealership. How does the staff treat you? How clean is the service department? Keep your ears and eyes open. Ask about extended hours, Saturday service, and loaner cars or shuttle service.

Ask the dealership about its customer service satisfaction index rating. Manufacturers survey all new car customers about their experiences with dealerships and produce ratings that you are entitled to see. Look for a minimum J.D. Powers rating in the high 80s or 90s.

Web sites offer a wealth of information for car buyers.

Online pricing sites:
Edmunds Publications: www.edmunds.com
Kelley Blue Book: www.kbb.com
Car Club: www.carclub.com

Sites that connect shoppers with a network of dealers:
www.carpoint.msn.com
www.autoweb.com
www.autobytel.com
www.autoconnect.com
www.autosite.com

For overall vehicle costs over time:
www.intellichoice.com

When to Buy

The longer a car sits on the lot, the more the dealer wants to get rid of it. Shopping at the end of the month will often help you drive a harder bargain. By shopping at the end of the calendar year, you may be able to save by buying this year's model.

Dealers will often place additional sales commissions on vehicles they want to get rid of. Salespeople may be eager to qualify for these commissions or to meet their minimum monthly quotas. In some cases, dealers may also be eligible for bonuses if they sell a specific number of cars within a specific period of time.

Test-Drive

No matter how you buy your next vehicle, in the flesh or online, you should test-drive the vehicle (or at least one with the exact same equipment). No legitimate dealership will deny you the right to a test-drive.

Let's face it, not every car will be a good fit.

❖

Leave the dog and kids with a sitter, have the time it takes, and keep the radio—and anyone else—tuned to low or no volume. Spend at least twenty minutes in the vehicle. Check out the interior, basic controls, storage space, access to the front and rear seats, and head and leg room in both.

Is it really as easy as they say to remove that minivan's rear seats or to operate that integrated child seat? Are the switches and power controls within comfortable reach? Adjust the seat, the mirrors, the steering wheel. Could you drive across the country in this vehicle if you had to? Do you feel right sitting in it? How is your outward vision?

Try to vary your drive—from crowded streets to open highways. Climb steep hills with the air-conditioning on. It is using some of the engine's power—is there enough? Be sure you drive the vehicle in reverse at some point. How's the visibility?

Make sure the engine response is adequate when you accelerate; do you have power in reserve? Do the brakes feel solid when you press the pedal? Your vehicle should respond quickly and precisely to every move. Check out interior noise levels, especially wind noise.

In bright daylight, examine the exterior carefully. Do the exterior panels (where the door meets the fender and so forth) line up evenly? Are the paint surfaces flawless and free of blemishes, scratches, and dents? How about the windshield. Is there any distortion? Keep asking yourself: Is this a vehicle I want to live with for the next few years?

Don't be offended if a salesperson asks to photocopy your driver's license before you take a test-drive. This is for the dealer's security—would you get into a vehicle with a complete stranger? Upon returning to the dealership, you can always ask for the copy to be destroyed.

A short test-drive can't duplicate all the driving conditions a vehicle will face. It might be worthwhile to rent a vehicle close to what you have in mind. A few days behind the wheel will tell you a lot. Perhaps this is the car of your dreams. Perhaps not.

Buy It—Don't Be Sold It

I am always amazed at the buying sources that recommend you approach the car-buying process as a war in which either you or the dealer can win but never both. It doesn't have to be that way. The more information you have before buying, the better you will be able to end up with a win for both you and the dealer.

First, you will need to find out what the manfacturer charged the dealer for the vehicle and its options. This will not be the dealer's "invoice price," since that will not show the "holdback allowance" (an additional amount the manufacturer pays the dealer when the vehicle is sold, usually 2 to 4 percent of the manufacturer's suggested retail price) or additional dealership incentives. *Edmund's New Car and Truck Buying Guides* will help you find the figure you need. A wealth of pricing information is also available on the Internet.

To help "move the metal," manufacturers provide rebates and incentives. A rebate goes directly to you as a reduction in the price of the car or as a lump sum cash payment. An incentive goes to the dealer, who can pass it along to you or not. Make a visit to your largest local library for a review of *Automotive News*, an industry publication that will help you determine dealer incentives.

Glossary of Buying Terms

DOHC, displacement, and *torque* are just a few of the many confusing terms and mysterious abbreviations you are likely to meet as you review the basics of engines, transmissions, and drivetrains. Here are some of those terms in non-technical language:

all-wheel-drive: a drivetrain configuration in which power goes to all four wheels, giving awesome traction on slippery surfaces as well as dry roads. Sometimes referred to as full-time all-wheel drive, this system has no two-wheel-drive mode.

automatic transmission: the most popular transmission and a godsend in city traffic. Look for a transmission that is electronically controlled and has a minimum of four speeds, including an "overdrive" gear. Computerized transmissions do the work of shifting gears seamlessly, while reducing "hunting," the tendency of a transmission to shift frequently from gear to gear as if it can't make up its mind.

brake horsepower: the amount of power produced by an engine at a given number of revolutions, taking into account the fan, rolling resistance of the tires, and back pressure from the exhaust.

cylinders: hollow metal tubes that contain pistons, round metal plugs that move up and down. More cylinders usually mean more power (and perhaps fewer miles to the gallon). Four-cylinder engines are popular and economical choices for compact and subcompact vehicles. But for engine smoothness as well as the acceleration needed for passing and merging, there is nothing quite like a well-made V-6 or V-8—or, if you have oodles of money, a V-10 or a V-12. V-6s and V-8s are great for towing or hauling heavy cargo.

engine displacement: the volume of air (expressed in liters or cubic inches) pushed out of the cylinders by the pistons on their upward strokes; a measure of engine size. In general, more displacement means more power.

four-wheel drive: a drivetrain configuration in which power can be transferred to all four wheels. Four-wheel-drive systems offer good grip in low-traction situations (a slippery boat ramp or snowy highway). Many offer a choice of two-wheel or four-wheel drive in response to different road conditions. Some offer a low gear for more severe off-road conditions.

front-wheel drive: a drivetrain configuration, originally designed to save space, in which power is transmitted only to the front wheels. The differential is moved forward and combined with the transmission to be called the transaxle. Placing the heavy engine and transmission over the driving wheels results in additional traction on wet or slippery road surfaces.

manual transmission: a transmission in which the driver determines gear selection by shifting a lever or "stick shift." If you enjoy the control that changing gears gives you, look for a car with a fifth gear for economical highway driving and silky smooth gear changes.

multivalve engines: engines with more than the traditional two valves per cylinder. Adding more valves helps an engine produce more power—by getting more fuel in and more burned gases out. Multivalve engines are usually named for the total number of valves. For example, a four-cylinder engine with four valves per cylinder is a 16 valve.

rack and pinion steering: a direct and lightweight steering system consisting of a pinion gear (with a small number of teeth) and a long rack with teeth; now considered standard

rear-wheel drive: a drivetrain configuration that transmits power from the engine to the rear wheels only, via a long turning bar called the driveshaft.

single overhead cams (SOHCs) and double overhead cams (DOHCs): camshafts, metal bars that operate the valves, that are positioned over the top of the cylinders rather than on the side (as in a traditional pushrod engine). Overhead cams have a more direct connection to the valves, which helps engines breathe and burn fuel more efficiently and powerfully. A double overhead camshaft (also called a twin cam) usually gives greater power.

torque: the rotational power of an engine. Maximum torque is measured at specific engine speeds and is expressed in pounds per foot. High torque at low speeds indicates good acceleration and is useful for towing. For most drivers, the wider the torque range the better.

turbochargers and superchargers: devices that add extra power to an engine by forcing it to breathe more air. They also usually require more frequent oil changes, along with special turbo-rated engine oil.

.Compare different dealers' best offers. *Automotive News* will also help you determine a car's "days supply," the volume of unsold cars. When the supply is over 60 to 70 days, it's a good bet that it's a buyer's market. *Car Deals*, 800/475-7283, offers more information.

For most vehicles, selling prices are negotiable, and buying is a lot like old-fashioned horse trading. Set a target buying price between the sticker price (manufacturer's suggested retail price) and the dealer "cost."

Your objective should be to determine what the dealership's lowest selling price would be. But don't discuss price until you are satisfied that this is an acceptable vehicle for you. If the salesperson asks what price it would take to "get you in the car today," politely tell him or her that you're approaching the buying process step by step and that settling on a price is a few steps ahead of where you are at the moment.

When you decide to negotiate, always begin from the dealer's cost up, not from the manufacturer's suggested retail price (MSRP) down. And be prepared to meet with some serious bargaining prowess. After all, these folks do this for a living.

Do not discuss your current vehicle until you agree on a price for the new one. Simply say you are not sure what you will do with the vehicle and that you are keeping your options open at the time.

When you have come to an agreement on price, you will usually go next to the Finance and Insurance (F&I) department. Here, you will be offered additional products and services such as rustproofing, credit insurance, and extended service contracts. Do not agree to any of these items unless you see the value. Are the benefits to you equal or greater than what the extras will cost you? Bring along a notebook and a calculator and double-check all charges in the same way you would a long grocery bill.

You can avoid most of this experience. Not everyone hates negotiating. There are car-buying brokers who promise, for a fee, to find the best price for the vehicle you're interested in. Or you can contact an online service such as Auto-by-Tel or AutoVantage. With both of these services—and there are more coming in the near future—you tell them the specific vehicle you are interested in, and they will get a local dealer to contact you with a firm price. Some on-line sites also will give you detailed information on pricing (MSRP and dealer cost) and rebates, road tests, quality evaluations, options, and warranties.

Your Old Car: Selling or Trading In

Unless you are buying your first new vehicle or giving your current car to a member of the family, you will need to make a decision about what to do with the car you currently own. You can trade it to the dealer who sells you your new car or you can sell it yourself outright. You will probably get more for your vehicle if you sell it on your own. But you will have to invest some time and elbow grease into the process. Regardless of how you handle the trade in or sale, you will need to determine the car's value beforehand.

Check the classified section of your local newspaper to find out the average price your vehicle is selling for. Call your bank or credit union or check with several publications at a bookstore or your local library. *Kelly's Blue Book*, (www.kbb.com) and the *National Auto Dealers Association Official Used Car Guide* have traditionally been the best sources for used car and truck values.

Whichever guide you use, be sure it lists both wholesale and trade-in values. Microsoft Car Point is another good source of information. Be sure as you search for listings that you take into account options like automatic transmission and air-conditioning, which can add or subtract substantially from the base value of your car.

Prepare your car for sale by washing and polishing the exterior and shampooing and vacuuming the interior. This is a good time to check the fluid levels and tire pressure. Gather all your maintenance receipts to show potential buyers that you have taken good care of your vehicle.

Decide where you will advertise—in the classified section of your local newspaper or in specialized classified publications. You may be able to post ads on business, community, and church bulletin boards. Be sure to prepare a good ad that stresses the strong points of your vehicle.

Caution: placing ads and handling the responses can be very time consuming. You will probably have interested parties coming to your home or garage. At some point, they are going to want to drive your vehicle. Do you really want to let a complete stranger drive away with your car, or worse yet accompany them? Maybe not—unless you have a relative or friend who's built like a bouncer and will handle these matters for you.

When you do make the sale, accept only cash or a cashier's check. And be sure to notify your insurance company immediately that you have sold your vehicle.

Should you take the quicker and easier route and trade-in your vehicle, expect to get only the wholesale value of the car. If possible, conclude the deal on the new vehicle with a firm price before discussing the trade-in.

Taking Delivery of Your Vehicle

Pick up your new vehicle during the day or in a well-lighted drive-through area so that you can carefully inspect it for any paint flaws or blemishes. The dealer should either fix these on the spot or with a "we owe you" promise in writing.

The salesperson or whoever delivers the vehicle will want to show you what's important under the hood and in the trunk, and where the jack and spare tire are located, along with their instructions.

Warranties

A warranty is like health insurance—you can never have enough of it. Remember, though, the big print giveth, but the small print taketh away.

"Warranty-ese" can be confusing. Warranties differ in mileage and time limits from one manufacturer to the next, even with individual brands from the same manufacturer. Some warranties can be applied to pre-owned vehicles. The following definitions can help:

Basic Vehicle Warranty: The basic new vehicle warranty covers everyting from the front license plate to the chrome-tipped exhaust pipe. Normal wear-and-tear items such as brakes and wipers are usually not covered. To correct manufacturer's blemishes, any dealer selling the same brand is required to make the necessary corrections at no cost to the owner. Makers of components like tires and batteries usually provide separate warranties that you should also review before you take delivery.

Powertrain Warranty: This warranty covers the "heavy" components (engine, transmission, and differential) that deliver power from the engine to the wheels. Powertrain warranties are usually longer in duration than basic new vehicle warranties because powertrain components are very reliable in modern cars. It is especially important to examine warranties on four-wheel and all-wheel-drive vehicles, which have more moving parts than two-wheel-drive vehicles.

Emissions Control Warranty: The federal government has mandated this special warranty, which covers any defective component or system (including the engine control computer) that could increase a car's harmful emissions. The term is for five years or 50,000 miles.

Corrosion or Rust-Through Warranty: Surface rust is generally not covered by this warranty but rust perforation caused by weather—natural elements—is. The old adage "a clean car runs better" works to keep you from claims on this warranty.

Extended Warranty: If you drive a lot of miles in a year or if you intend to keep your vehicle a long time, this warranty may be worth considering. It costs extra, and plans vary considerably. Essentially, you are extending the basic warranty beyond its time and mileage period. Consider only manufacturer-backed extended warranties. As with all warranties, read the plan carefully. Ask the following questions: What is covered? What is specifically not covered? How much do I pay for each claim? Is there a deductible or copayment? Do I have to use a specific repair organization or am I free to choose any one?

Roadside Assistance Plans: Anything from offering aid when you've locked your keys in the car to bringing gasoline when you've run out or changing a flat tire (see chapter 16 about how to do this yourself)—that's what a roadside plan will do. A roadside plan is offered by most manufacturers these days. Compare manufacturers' offerings, as they can differ widely.

Leasing

Approximately one-third of all new cars are now leased. Despite the fact that leasing is usually more expensive than buying the same vehicle outright, it is sometimes the smart way to go. It's a good way to drive a new vehicle every few years, usually with smaller monthly payments than you'll have with traditional financing and relatively little up-front cash, particularly if the lease is subsidized by the manufacturer. Leasing is also a good way to avoid the hassle of repair bills.

Leasing may very well be the way to get your hands on the automobile of your dreams. But before you sign on the dotted line, know all your obligations. Leasing contracts vary considerably and can be confusing. Knowing the ins and outs of leasing can help you to avoid problems.

Step I: Don't wait until the end of the model year to lease. As the year goes on, you are likely to find higher monthly payments in response to increasing vehicle prices and lower residuals (estimated value of the vehicle at the end of the lease).

Step II: Be prepared to bargain. Determine what the dealer paid for the vehicle and its options and establish your target price for the vehicle just as you would when buying.

Step III: Get it all in writing. Get the complete cost of the lease from the lessor in writing—every dime that you will have to spend, including all state taxes and fees. There may be a fee to have the dealer initiate the lease (acquisition fee), and if you don't purchase the vehicle at the end of the lease, there may be a fee to dispose of the vehicle (a disposition fee), as well as others. Highlight anything you're not clear about and ask questions until you understand, or have a lawyer read the lease before you sign.

Step IV: Determine depreciation. Most cars lose their value over time, and depreciation happens at different rates for different vehicles. The cost of the lease is figured on the difference between the manufacturer's suggested retail price (MSRP) at the beginning of the lease and the car's market value (what the dealer can sell the car for) at the end of the lease.

Step V: Close the lease. Determine the value of the vehicle at the end of the lease (its fair market value) before you sign. Most leases are close-ended, but be sure that the amount is in the written contract. Without this agreed-to number, you have an "open-ended lease." If you decide to buy the vehicle at the end of the lease, you may not like the lessor's assessment of the vehicle's value.

Step VI: Plan ahead for a mutually beneficial relationship. You must return the vehicle to the dealership from which you leased it, but you don't have to buy or lease from them again unless you have had a good leasing experience. If you are not satisfied with the service you received, you can arrange a lease with another dealership before you actually return the vehicle.

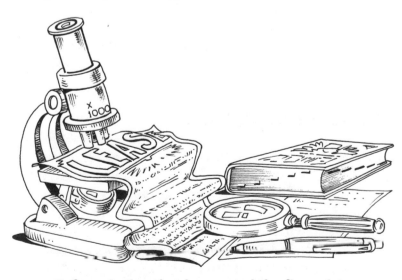

Before signing that lease, read the fine print.

Step VII: Maintain your vehicle. Know what maintenance the manufacturer requires and provide for it. You may be faced with an additional charge at the end of the lease if the vehicle you return has excessive wear and tear. You can be charged for a damaged fender, worn tires, and bad brakes. Parking-lot dings and dents, as long as they are minor, are generally not charged to you. If possible, get a specific definition of "abnormal" or "excessive" wear before you sign.

Step VIII: Understand early termination penalties. Most leases are for two to four years. Plan on keeping the vehicle for the entire term. Determine what early termination penalties will apply if you have to end the lease early. Make certain that you have the option of early termination or converting your present lease into another.

Step IX: Watch out for excess mileage. Determine how much you drive in a year. If there is any possibility that you will exceed the 12,000- or 15,000-mile cap, think twice. The premium for this excess can be 10 to 20 cents per mile. You may be able to find a lease that permits high mileage for a reasonable cost.

Step X: Carefully evaluate the extended warranty. New cars come with a basic warranty, usually three years, 36,000 miles, or longer. An extended warranty picks up where the basic drops off. If you're only keeping the vehicle the length of the lease, you don't need an extended warranty.

Leasing has both risks and rewards. Make certain that you understand both before you sign on the dotted line.

Pre-owned Vehicles

There are many reasons why buying a used vehicle may be a Car Smart decision for you: 1) the high cost of new cars and trucks, 2) the loss of value, or depreciation, that many vehicles suffer as soon as you drive them off the dealer's lot, 3) the reliability and long life of modern used vehicles, 4) the increasing number of well-made, well-maintained, low-mileage vehicles coming off lease.

As with buying a new vehicle, your process should

When purchasing a pre-owned vehicle, arrange for a thorough inspection.

❖

include a practical needs analysis and setting a budget that you can afford. Manufacturer's literature may not be readily available, so you will have to look to other sources. Fortunately, there are several that can help you locate a used car or truck that will provide you with many trouble-free miles.

Read the car-buff magazines to narrow your choices to a few. Through your local library or bookstore, check out *Consumer Reports Buying Guide* "Frequency of Repair Ratings" or *Kiplinger Report*'s automotive issue. These publications will help you identify any known trouble spots. Both publications also recommend specific used makes and models and advises avoiding others. With all this data at hand, you can reduce many of the traditional risks associated with buying "someone else's problems."

Having found a vehicle that suits your needs, whether it's from a dealership, a used car superstore, or a private individual, pay to have a professional repair shop inspect it with a fine-toothed comb. That inspection should also include the body of the vehicle to determine if the car has been in an accident. If your research has turned up any known trouble spots with the model, alert the inspector to those. Expect to pay for approximately one hour of labor for the inspection. Be certain to agree on a price *prior* to the inspection.

Certified Pre-owned Vehicles

Many manufacturers assist dealers in selling pre-owned vehicles by establishing a certification process. Vehicles in these programs are inspected thoroughly, repaired, and reconditioned before they are sold. Some are even backed by extended factory warranties and roadside assistance programs. You may pay more up front, but you're likely to save a lot on repair bills. The certification process varies from manufacturer to manufacturer. So read the fine print before you buy.

Whether you're shopping for a new or pre-owned vehicle, the key to a successful buying or leasing experience is research and legwork. Now that you've found that right vehicle, let's look at what it takes to make certain it will run smoothly and reliably, to minimize repairs, and to extend its useful life as long as possible.

3
AIR AND FUEL: THE DIET, PARTS 1 AND 2

This chapter describes how the car's "diet" of air and fuel is delivered to the engine and includes tips on how you can avoid expensive repairs to fuel injectors. It's all you ever wanted to know but were afraid to ask about gasoline, including how to choose the right fuel for your vehicle.

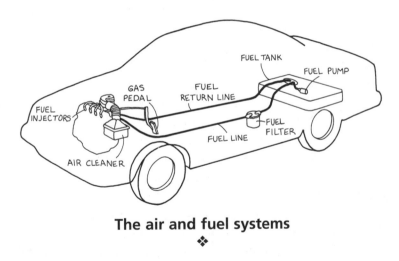

The air and fuel systems

❖

Carburetor was just one of the "secret" words that was knowingly thrown around by my brothers as they poked their heads under the hoods of the cars parked in front of our home. It was as if there were a secret club, and I was not a member. When I finally learned what a carburetor is and what it does, I discovered it was no big secret, and there was no exclusive club.

A car's air-intake system is analagous to the lungs. The fuel-intake system can be likened to the mouth.

How Carburetors and Fuel Injectors Work

The definition of carburetion is "to combine chemically," and for many years, the carburetor was the system of choice for combining the first two parts of the engine's diet: air and fuel. In recent years, though, carburetors have been replaced by **fuel injectors**, the carburetor's faster and more efficient computerized cousin. Most vehicles built today are equipped with **fuel injection**. This does the same job as a carburetor but provides more power while permitting the engine to run on a mixture that is both cleaner (friendlier to the environment) and leaner (uses less fuel in proportion to air).

The carburetor is actually a food blender for your car's engine. It draws measured amounts of air from outside the car and combines it, in a very special way, with measured amounts of gasoline drawn from a tank in the rear of the car (as far away from the engine's spark as possible). This mixture is then distributed to the cylinders, the stomach of the engine.

In the carburetor, the liquid gasoline is transformed into a fine spray, similar to the mist produced by an atomizer. By making the gasoline molecules smaller, the carburetor turns the gasoline into a vapor.

Vaporized gas, which burns more easily than gasoline in its liquid form, is exactly what the doctor ordered. When vaporized gasoline burns, its heated gases explode and expand, pushing the pistons down. This causes the crankshaft to spin and the wheels to turn, and is the "combustion" in the internal combustion engine.

In the carburetor, liquid gasoline is transformed into a fine mist. In this new form, gasoline burns more easily.

Electronic Fuel Injection

There are two types of electronic fuel injection (EFI): throttle body and multi-port. **Throttle body fuel injection** looks like a souped-up carburetor that is missing its insides. It sprays a common measure of the fuel down to the engine, where it is distributed along a spray bar to each cylinder in equal amounts.

In **multi-port fuel injection**, a separate injector acts like a hypodermic needle, squirting a small amount of fuel into each cylinder. To give you some idea of how miserly this fuel metering system is, consider the microscopic hole through which the fuel is delivered. It's about the width of a human hair, and so tiny it has to be made with a laser beam! Even if you have thick hair, that's a very small opening. Nevertheless, the result is more power and less pollution.

A whiz-bang on-board computer, an electronic brain, is responsible for ensuring the success of the fuel injection system. This microprocessor, often called an electro-

The fuel injector opening is about the width of a human hair.

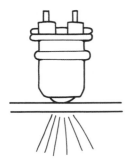

THROTTLE BODY
TYPE INJECTION

MULTI – PORT
TYPE INJECTION

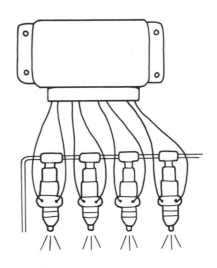

Throttle body and multi-port fuel injection are the two types of fuel injection found in today's cars.

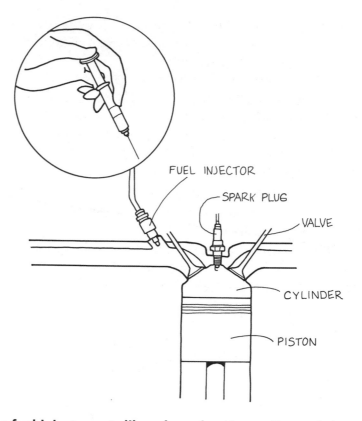

FUEL INJECTOR

SPARK PLUG

VALVE

CYLINDER

PISTON

The fuel injector acts like a hypodermic needle, squirting a tiny amount of fuel into each cylinder.

❖

nic control unit (ECU), receives information from **sensors** (electronic eyes and ears) located throughout the car. The sensors feed back information about many things, including the speed of the engine, the temperature of the air, and the density of the air and gasoline. With this input, the computer then determines the best ratio of air and fuel. To learn more about how these computers work, turn to chapter 8.

Air Filter

Cars require an enormous amount of air to breathe. About 9,000 gallons of air are needed for every one gallon of gasoline used. By anyone's reckoning, that's a lot.

It is important for the smooth running and long life of your car that the air it breathes is clean, that is, free of dirt and dust. It is the job of the appropriately named "air cleaner" to do just that.

A breather hose, commonly called a snorkel, actually carries the air from outside the car into the air cleaner. En route, it is heated by hot air that has been redirected from the engine by the **pre-heated air-intake** system. The air passes through the air cleaner, a container that houses the **air filter**—the workhorse of this cleanup detail. The air filter, which is made of pleated folds of paper, catches dirt and dust before it can get down into the finely machined engine parts.

Just like any home furnace filter, the air filter must be changed when it's full. Most cars need a new filter about once a year, every 15,000 miles (24,000 kilometers), or whenever your owner's manual recommends. If you happen to live in the Sahara, or merely on an extremely dusty road, you will probably want to change your air filter more often.

For years the air filter could be easily found under the hood. Checking and changing the filter was the classic do-it-yourself chore. Anyone who wanted to save a trip to the repair shop could check the air filter merely by

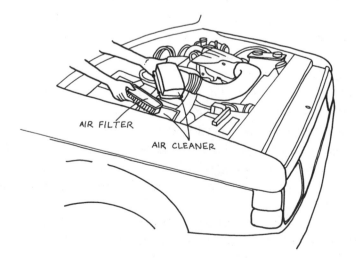

AIR FILTER

AIR CLEANER

Most cars need a new air filter about once a year.

A dirty air filter can increase fuel consumption by 10 percent.

removing a couple of clamps and performing a simple test. You would just remove the filter and hold it up to a light; if light could be seen coming through one side, the filter was still in good shape.

As hood designs have been lowered, though, air filters are now found in a wide range of sizes, shapes, and colors and are located in several different areas within the engine compartment. Some manufacturers now advise that the air filter should only be removed by a trained professional. They warn that the flow of air to the engine may be interrupted if the filter is positioned incorrectly when it is replaced. If the airflow is interrupted, the car may run roughly or not at all. A few dollars savings may turn into ten times that much spent on a visit to the repair shop to correct the problem.

If do-it-yourself isn't dead, it sure is breathing hard!

How Fuel Is Fed to the Engine

To get the gasoline from the rear of the car to the engine, a **fuel pump** (usually more than one), located either in the gas tank or between the tank and the engine, pushes the gasoline along the **fuel lines**, which lie along the bottom of the car. Until the 1970s, fuel pumps were mechanically driven by an attachment to the turning engine. The majority of fuel pumps manufactured today are electric. Within the tank there is also a device called a **sending unit** that monitors the amount of gasoline and sends that information in the form of electronic impulses to the gas gauge located on the dashboard.

On its way to the engine, the gasoline passes through one or more **fuel filters**, miniature versions of the air filter, which catch dirt and foreign particles before they reach the working parts of the carburetor or fuel injectors.

A fuel filter may be small, but it's mighty. This tiny filter is responsible for cleaning the many gallons of gasoline that pass through it and should be changed regularly to ensure peak performance. The fuel filter in

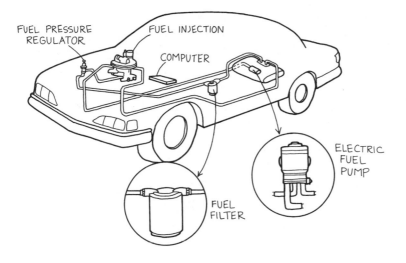

Fuel is fed to the engine by a fuel pump, which pushes gasoline along the fuel lines to the fuel injector.

❖

most cars should be changed about once a year, every 10,000 miles, or whenever your owner's manual says.

Important Facts About Fuel

As teenagers, my five brothers and I used the family car, so it was common in our house to hear Dad yelling as he slammed the front door, "Who used the damn car last? And why didn't you put gas in it?" Mercifully, often by the time he recited the litany of all our names, he had forgotten the infraction. There's no telling how many times he was stranded because of our selective reading of the gas gauge.

After I graduated from school, I began driving my first car. It was a little black Volkswagen that I dearly loved and still remember fondly. And it taught me a lot about gasoline.

Despite the fact that my Bug got about 172 miles to the gallon, I habitually refused to put in more than 47 cents worth of gas at any one time. This had much to do with the fact that I never seemed to have more than 47 cents to spend at one time. Furthermore, using the skills I had learned as a teenager, I meticulously estimated exactly how much gas was in the tank at any given time. Using these calculations, I frequently arrived at a gas station with little more than fumes in the tank. The car would struggle, sputter, cough, and die in front of the pump, and I would emerge triumphant, congratulating myself for doing another swell job of squeezing every last drop out of the tank. I then pumped in another 47 cents worth and off I'd go for two more weeks. It was not until several years later that I discovered what my calculations had really wrought.

Now, take a look at the illustration of the fuel tank. See those little dots at the bottom of the gas tank? Those harm-

**As a teenager, I perfected the art of running on empty . . .
and had no idea what it was doing to my beloved Bug.**

❖

less-looking specks are actually pieces of dirt and contaminants that gradually accumulate at the bottom of any gas tank. The particles rest there, harmless, until the fuel level in the tank gets so low that the fuel pump sucks them out along with the last few drops of gasoline.

To continue the story, every time I arrived at the station with the gauge on "empty," the dirt and other contaminants at the bottom of the tank had been forced along the fuel lines to the fuel filter, which quickly clogged and needed replacement. As a result, I bought a lot of unnecessary fuel filters and paid for several tows and a carburetor cleanout!

Even after I discovered the expensive consequences of my 47-cent habit, I couldn't seem to quit. Desperate, I

Money-Saving Tip

If you live in a cold climate, avoid **gas line freeze-up** by keeping your gas tank as full as possible, especially at night. Condensation causes water droplets to form inside the gas tank. On days when the temperature drops below freezing, water droplets can turn into ice crystals that move along the gas line with the gas and clog the flow of gasoline. The less space in the tank, the less area in which condensation can form. Be particularly careful during the spring and fall months when condensation is increased by greater daytime-to-nighttime temperature fluctuations.

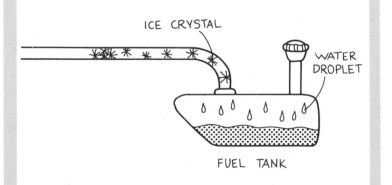

On very cold days, water droplets in the gas tank can turn into ice crystals that move along the gas line with the gas and clog the flow of gasoline.

Pieces of dirt and contaminants accumulate at the bottom of the gas tank and are pumped out to the fuel injectors along with the last few drops of gasoline. The moral? Gas is not "good 'til the last drop."

began to pretend that if the tank showed a quarter of a tank, it was actually empty. I am happy to say I am finally cured. Now I habitually practice the second nicest thing anyone can do for a car: keep the tank as full as possible. (I'll tell you the first nicest thing you can do for your car in chapter 9.) Remember, gas is not "good 'til the last drop."

Choosing the Right Gasoline

The **octane rating** of a gasoline (the number displayed on the side of the gas pump) refers to its resistance to **knocking** or **pinging**. Ideally, gasoline should burn smoothly and evenly throughout the entire combustion chamber. If the gasoline has too low an octane number, it may burn roughly or explode at the wrong time, subjecting the engine to vibration. The engine will still run, but it will wear more quickly.

The sound you may hear coming from the engine is a metallic rattling that is called pinging or knocking. It sounds like metal marbles or ball bearings rattling around together. The higher the octane, the slower and smoother the gasoline will burn and the less likely it is to burn irregularly and cause knocking or pinging.

Should you buy super unleaded gasoline? Not necessarily. To know for sure if you should be paying the extra

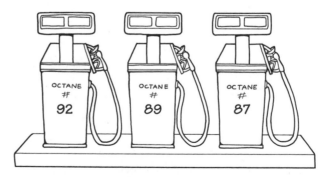

The octane rating of a gasoline refers to its resistance to knocking or pinging. The higher the octane, the smoother the gasoline will burn.

Gasoline that has too low an octane rating may burn roughly or explode at the wrong time.

❖

cents per gallon for premium unleaded, read your owner's manual. If you find it recommends premium unleaded, or a gas with an equivalent octane rating, use it. The manufacturer's advice is based on its extensive experience with your engine. In other words, like it or not, your car's engine may simply require the more expensive premium unleaded gas for engine performance that is knock- or ping-free. But if your owner's manual recommends the use of regular or mid-grade, don't bother with the higher priced gas.

If you're already using premium unleaded and you still hear pinging or knocking, it's a good idea to have the car checked out by a professional. Some pinging is normal in newer cars and is considered an acceptable trade-off for the fuel efficiency. Excessive pinging or knocking, however, can cause engine damage. If there's any question in your mind about your car's ping, rattle, or knock, ask your service provider to decide by road testing your car.

Alternative Technology

It would take approximately 25 of today's cleaner burning cars to pollute the planet as much as just one

Your car may knock or ping if you choose a gasoline with an octane rating that is too low.

Frequently asked questions

Q How do I calculate my car's fuel economy?

A Divide mileage by gallons of gas. For instance, if you traveled 300 miles on 10 gallons, your car's fuel economy is 30 miles per gallon.

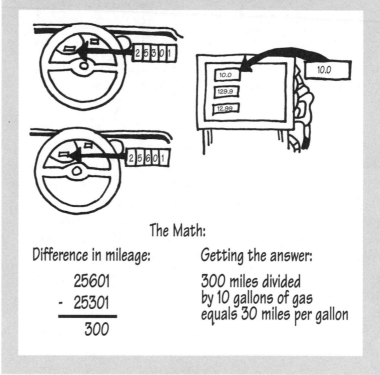

The Math:

Difference in mileage:

$$25601$$
$$-\ 25301$$
$$\overline{300}$$

Getting the answer:

300 miles divided
by 10 gallons of gas
equals 30 miles per gallon

Tip:

Tracking fuel economy is like keeping a finger on your car's pulse. A drop in fuel economy over a short time might mean that a visit to your service provider is in order.

pre–emission control vehicle of the 1950s or 1960s. Nevertheless, pollution from vehicles remains a growing concern for society, government, and the automotive industry.

One solution is to modify gasoline so that it burns more cleanly. Adding oxygen to gasoline causes it to burn more completely, and more cleanly. Currently, several new oxygenated fuels are available. Among the most popular additions are **ethanol** and **MTBE**. Ethanol is organically based; it's made from grain. MTBE is synthetic; it's made in a chemical laboratory. Note: As

long as the additives in these specially formulated fuels
are found in proportions approved by the manufacturer
(check your owner's manual), they should be harmless to
your car and friendly to the environment.

Alternatives to gasoline include methanol, made
from natural gas or biomass (wood chips or garbage),
compressed natural gas, and liquid petroleum gas, also
known as propane. High cost, engineering problems,
public relunctance, and, in some cases, an inadequate
distribution system are just some of the hurdles encoun-
tered when alternative fuels are introduced to the mar-
ketplace.

Federal and state clean air laws are also spurring
automakers, in collaboration with national labs, auto
suppliers, and universities, to develop innovative, high-
mileage, low-emission alternatives to the internal combustion engine. Several environmentally friendly
technologies are promising, but it is not certain which of
them will propel motorists into the future.

The most likely alternative appears to be a hybrid
vehicle. Hybrids combine two energy sources. In some

New oxygenated fuels burn cleaner—that is, pollute less.

cases, the dual power sources take turns powering the vehicle; in others they operate simultaneously.

A typical hybrid has a combustion engine (gas turbine, diesel engine) or fuel cell for long-range driving and an electric motor for stop-and-go city driving (and ultra-low emissions). In some systems, the engine shuts down when the vehicle is at rest or decelerating. During acceleration and hill climbing, both the engine and the electric motor work together to provide power.

Many electric hybrid vehicles use an innovative system called regenerative braking. Unlike conventional braking systems, in which motion energy is lost as heat at the brake pads, regenerative braking systems partially recharge a vehicle's batteries when the driver uses the brakes.

Frequently asked questions

Q What is "vapor lock"?

A The additives in today's gasoline have raised their **volatility**, which is the ability to change from a liquid to a vapor. During hot weather, gasoline may actually boil, causing it to stop flowing. The result is **vapor lock**: the engine is deprived of fuel, and lets you know with symptoms such as rough running, loss of power, and, in some instances, stalling.

Modern electric fuel pumps located far from the heat of the engine provide more constant pressure to the system and have alleviated the problem in most cars. But if yours isn't one of those, and vapor lock is a problem, try switching from your regular brand of gasoline to another reputable brand. If that doesn't work, it's possible that the fuel lines can be rerouted so they are farther removed from the hot spots of the engine.

Nickel Metal Hydride Batteries

One of the greatest roadblocks to the development of electric vehicles with low emissions and greater fuel economy has been inadequate battery power. Traditional lead acid batteries are heavy, slow to recharge, and shorted-lived. While there have been significant advances in lead acid batteries and some promising results with lithium-ion batteries, the battery technology that is currently showing the most promise is the nickel metal hydride battery.

Nickel metal hydride batteries work by storing and releasing hydrogen ions during the charging and discharging processes. They have double the energy of lead-acid batteries by weight, so they can move electric vehicles farther (in some cases doubling the vehicle's range). The batteries are maintenance free and recyclable, and they have better cold-weather performance and more durability than lead-acid batteries.

Nickel metal hydride batteries have been used for years in laptop computers, cellular phones, and video products. The challenge for engineers is to use these batteries to provide electric vehicles with about 70 times the energy of the average laptop. Currently, nickel metal hydride batteries are several times more expensive to produce than smaller consumer batteries.

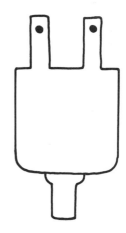

Electric vehicles draw their energy from battery packs.

Fuel Cell Engines

Fuel cells are one of the most likely candidates to revolutionize the manufacture and storage of energy. A fuel cell hybrid electric vehicle draws primary energy from an onboard fuel cell and supplemental energy from batteries.

Like a battery, a fuel cell generates electricity from a chemical reaction. In other words, it converts fuel (gasoline, methanol, or hydrogen) into power for an electric motor or other system without combustion. A fuel cell yields proportionately higher energy than an internal combustion engine and produces almost none of the pollutants traditionally associated with burning fuel.

Fuel cell technology is already used to generate

electricity for industrial and consumer use and in the aerospace industry. But for widespread acceptance, fuel cell cost and weight must be further reduced.

Look Ma, No Hands!

Next-generation transportation may also include automated highway systems (AHS). In these systems, magnets embedded in the pavement and electromagnetometers in cars will be used to guide vehicles. Computer controlled engines, brakes, and steering systems; adaptive cruise control that uses radar and infrared technology; and other devices will regulate speed and distances between vehicles.

Drivers on automated highway systems will have a hands-free driving experience. Eventually, drivers won't even need to operate the brake pedal or the accelerator. While it may not be as much fun as driving today, you sure could catch up on your reading.

One thing seems likely: the lightweight, high-mileage, ultra-low emission vehicles of the future will probably involve new fuels, inventive energy storage, strong ultralight metals like magnesium, low-rolling-resistance tires, sophisticated exhausts, and aerodynamics that approach that of an airplane. Whatever the alternatives to today's internal combustion gasoline engines, they will have to be cleaner and more fuel-efficient, while still affordable, safe, and comfortable.

For more information on alternative fuel and technology, check out the U.S. Department of Energy's Web site: www.ott.doe.gov/.

Making your car go the distance
Fuel Delivery System

If you follow a few simple rules, you'll help your fuel delivery systems last. Preventive maintenance with these systems is essential.

✓ Air and fuel filters trap dirt and dust and must be changed when they are full. Most cars need a new air and fuel filter about once a year, every 15,000 miles (24,000 kilometers), or whenever your owner's manual recommends.

✓ The microscopic openings of fuel injectors require squeaky clean gasoline. To avoid fuel-related performance problems, buy a reputable brand of gasoline to be sure that you're getting the best quality detergents.

✓ Try changing gasoline brands to solve minor engine performance problems. The additive packages of each major brand are different, and some cars "like" one better than another. After you fill up, look for any change, for better or worse, in the way the car drives.

✓ Fuel injectors and carburetors need periodic cleaning and/or adjustment. But hire a trained specialist equipped with up-to-date equipment and service manuals to work on your fuel injectors. Check your owner's manual for service schedule specifics.

Troubleshooting the Air and Fuel Systems

Possible causes →

Symptoms	Dirty air filter	Cold enrichment system	Dirty/faulty carburetor	Dirty/faulty fuel injectors	Fuel pressure*	Contaminated fuel	Incorrect octane	Air (vacuum) leak	Vapor lock/hot soak	Idle speed control system	Computer-related**	Fuel leak
No start / hard start–cold	●	●	●	●	●	●		●		●		
Hard start–hot	●		●	●	●			●	●			
Stalling / hesitation–warm	●		●	●	●	●		●	●	●		
Stalling/hesitation–cold	●	●	●	●				●		●	●	
Rough idle	●		●	●	●	●		●		●	●	
High idle			●					●		●	●	
Surging			●	●	●			●			●	
Knocking/pinging (on acceleration)						●	●				●	
Afterfire (dieseling)			●	●		●	●					
Backfire			●				●					
Poor fuel economy	●		●	●							●	
Black smoke/tailpipe	●	●	●	●							●	
Lack of power	●		●	●	●			●			●	
"Check engine" light on				●	●			●		●	●	
Gas fumes			●						●			●

*Fuel pump pressure could be fuel filter, fuel pump, fuel pump pickup, fuel pressure regulator, fuel pump drain valve, restricted fuel line.

**Computer-related symptoms can be caused by the computer itself, its wiring and connection, or one of many sensors including mass air flow sensor, coolant sensor, throttle position sensor, crankshaft sensor, oxygen sensor and many others not listed here. Before beginning computer diagnosis the technician should inspect the engine, mechanical, electrical, and fuel systems.

4
THE SPARK: IGNITION AND CHARGING

The ignition and charging systems provide the spark that gets a car started and keeps it going. This chapter describes how these systems work and makes recommendations that can help ensure that your car starts every time, runs more reliably, and gets better fuel economy. You'll learn about the life and death of batteries, what a tune-up is, and when to get one.

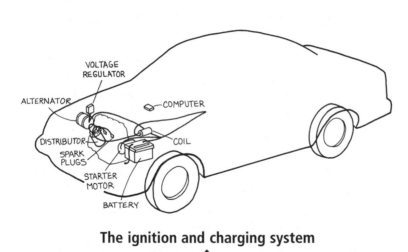

The ignition and charging system
❖

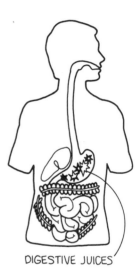

DIGESTIVE JUICES

The ignition system can be compared to the human body's digestive system: both break down the components of a diet, and both release energy that is converted into motion.

"Ignition," once I had learned its meaning, was another automotive term that convinced me that cars were not mysterious. Ignition comes from the word *ignite*, to set on fire, and what better device for setting something on fire than a spark? The job of your car's ignition system, therefore, is to add a spark to the explosive air and fuel

The igniting spark journeys from the battery to the coil and on to the distributor, where it is "dealt" to the spark plugs. There the spark ignites the air/fuel mixture.

❖

mixture that the fuel delivery system has taken such pains to create.

How the Ignition System Works

The journey of the spark begins at the **battery** and ends at the **spark plug**. If anything interrupts it along the route, the car will not start at all, will start with difficulty, or will run roughly.

When you turn the ignition key, it sends a wake-up call to a small (12 volts) electrical **current** that has been resting in the battery. Those 12 volts aren't much in electrical terms (your home generally uses 110 and 220 volts), but before their journey is over, they will have been magnified many thousands of times.

When activated by the ignition key's wake-up call, the small particles within the battery begin to move around in a solution of water and chemicals called **electrolyte.** It is this movement that will be converted into electrical energy, or current.

From the battery, the 12 volts travel to the **coil,** where they get a big boost. The coil turns those puny 12 volts into a fortified spark—40,000 to 50,000 volts of electricity. That's enough voltage to curl your hair without a curling iron.

From the coil, the spark moves to the **distributor**, which acts like a card dealer. The distributor deals an equal portion of the spark to each cylinder. There a spark plug receives the spark. This very hot spark now jumps, or **arcs**, across the gap at the tip of the spark plug. The spark flashes, causing the air/fuel mixture to explode. *Kaboom! Kapow! Kapooey!* The spark's entire journey, from battery to spark plug, takes place in a fraction of a second!

Getting a Good Start

At the same time the ignition key is sending a message to the battery, it is also sending another signal to the **starter**. This small but powerful electrical motor starts things off by moving the pistons up and down until the first explosion takes place and the engine turns over.

The starter's distinctive feature is a small, round, metal-toothed wheel, or **gear**. Attached to this gear is an

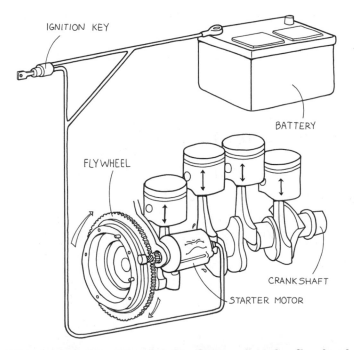

The starter gets things going by turning the flywheel, which turns the crankshaft, which moves the pistons up and down.

arm called a **solenoid**. When the ignition key is turned to "on," the solenoid pushes the gear forward so that it meshes with a large heavy disc called the **flywheel**. The flywheel is attached to the **crankshaft**, the metal bar that holds onto the pistons. The flywheel also has teeth in the form of its **ring gear**. When the flywheel turns, the crankshaft turns. When the crankshaft turns, the pistons move up and down.

As soon as the flywheel begins to turn, the starter's job is finished. It pulls itself back and away from the rapidly turning flywheel in order to avoid decapitation!

At a time when electricity is pretty much taken for granted, electric starters hardly seem worthy of special notice, but without them, our automotive lives would look very different. Think about this: Before modern starters were invented, cars were started by manually turning a metal bar or crank that fit into a socket in the engine. It was often necessary to repeat this back-breaking task many times—50 to 150 hand cranks were not uncommon—before the engine would start. An incorrect grip or a backfire, causing the crank to jump back on the cranker, could result in a broken thumb, arm, or jaw, with an occasional hernia thrown in for good measure.

Money-Saving Tip

To keep its electrical system healthy, give your car a break from stop-and-go traffic and drive it for 20 to 30 minutes at highway speeds. Doing this once a week revitalizes the charging system. It's the equivalent of giving your car a good aerobic workout.

The Charging System

A battery doesn't make electricity; it only stores it—much like a checking account stores dollars. Once the battery gets the engine running, the **alternator** takes over.

The alternator generates the electricity that provides power to all the electrical systems in the car while the engine is running. The alternator also sends to or "deposits" power in the battery while the car is running to recharge the battery's depleted electrical supply. In this way, the battery is always ready to start your car.

The **voltage regulator** acts as an auditor, controlling the flow of electrical power to and from these devices and ensuring that the battery is neither discharged nor overcharged by the alternator.

As is true of many of the components in your car, the alternator is activated by a belt that runs on a pulley, similar to a clothesline pulley. The belt is attached to the turning crankshaft. Whenever the engine is running, the belt turns and the alternator makes electricity to recharge the battery and to power the accessories. However, the alternator only fully recharges the battery when the car has been driven for approximately 5 to 20 minutes at highway speeds.

The charging system works like a checking account: the battery stores and "spends" electricity, the alternator makes deposits of electrical current, and the voltage regulator audits the flow.

Belts

Cars have from one to five belts under the hood. Many newer cars have a single **serpentine** belt that drives all the accessories. Belts transfer power from the engine to various components, including the alternator, water

Frequently asked questions

Q What should I do if the alternator light comes on?

A The good news is it's probably not fatal—just massively inconvenient. The rule is to keep driving until you reach a service station. Turn off as many electricity-draining accessories as you safely can. The hardest thing the electrical system has to do is start the car, so *don't turn the engine off unless it's absolutely necessary.*

Warning! If the temperature light comes on at the same time the alternator light is on (or simply by itself), stop the car as soon as you can. The same belt that drives the alternator often drives the water pump. If the water pump stops working, it won't be long before the engine overheats and its internal parts melt. The result will be major damage and expensive repairs.

An activated alternator or battery light means more electricity is being used than is being replaced.

pump, power steering pump, and the air conditioner. As
belts wear, they stretch and get thinner. As the thinner
belt sinks deeper into the pulley, you may hear a high-
pitched squeaking sound or a squeal (an extended version of a squeak) coming from under the hood. Incorrect
tension causes the belt to wear faster, and may cause the
component it drives to malfunction.

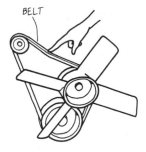

**Belts transfer
power from the
engine to various
components.**

Computerized Ignitions

Today almost all cars have **electronic computerized ignitions**. The same engine computer that provides a better
air/fuel mixture has also taken over coordinating the
functions of the traditional ignition system. Many of the
traditional ignition components, including the coil and
the distributor, have been replaced by electronic components. Sensors feed back information to the computer so
that it can determine when the spark should arrive and
how hot it should be when it gets there. (For more about
computers, see chapter 8.)

The Tune-up

A tune-up is the routine replacement of spark plugs,
filters, and other air-, fuel-, and ignition-related parts,
plus a precise series of tests and adjustments to regain

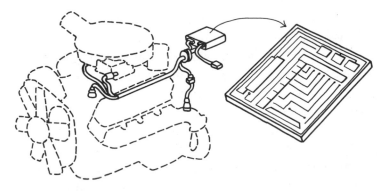

Almost all cars today have computerized ignitions.

Today's tune-up includes a computerized engine analysis that uses hundreds of tests to compare the car's performance with the manufacturer's standards.

maximum engine performance and fuel economy. For today's cars, this includes a computerized engine analysis that uses hundreds of tests to compare the car's performance with the manufacturer's standards.

Depending on whether it's minor or major, a tune-up may also include battery service, timing adjustment, idle speed adjustment, vacuum and compression checks, pollution control systems inspection, and the inspection of belts and hoses. What is included will depend on the make, model, and year of your vehicle, but the result should always be a quick-starting, smooth-running engine that gets the best possible fuel economy.

A tune-up does not include an oil change (or even an oil check!), nor does it include a brake inspection, tire rotation, wiper blade replacement—or tightening the screws on your license plate. While you may find it very desirable to get these maintenance chores done at the same time you get a tune-up, you will probably have to ask for them.

You won't find this information under the heading of "tune-up" in your owner's manual. (What you *will* find is a list of things all good car owners ought to do every so many weeks, months, years, or miles/kilometers—otherwise known as "scheduled service.") If the service in question directly concerns returning your car's engine to maximum operating performance (air, fuel, and spark), it is probably part of a tune-up.

The Life and Death of Batteries

As with most things in life, a battery ages and grows tired with use. The chemicals in the electrolyte are eventually absorbed into the interior walls or **plates** of the battery, where they form a hard, crusty deposit. These deposits first appear as a white powdery substance on the terminals that protrude from the battery's top or side. Eventually these deposits block the passage of the electrical current.

When the plates become completely covered, the battery discharges and can no longer provide the necessary electrical energy to start the car. If the battery is not too far gone, an electrical current is run through it in the

Money-Saving Tip

Batteries should be recharged slowly whenever possible. Incorrectly recharging a battery can destroy both the battery and expensive electronic accessories such as digital clocks.

opposite direction (a charging direction) by a battery charger, and the deposits disappear from the plates and return to the electrolyte. The battery may get a new life.

Eventually, however, all batteries die when they run out of chemicals, the plate deposits become too extensive, the plates vibrate and break apart, or the outside casing cracks.

Batteries also hate the cold. When the outside temperature is 80° F (27° C), a battery is 100 percent efficient. On a cold day, that same battery at 0° F (-18° C) is only 40 percent efficient. At -20° F (-29° C) it is only 18 percent efficient. In other words, more than 80 percent of its ability to store the electricity needed to start the car is temporarily absent! Just as important, when the temperature drops below freezing, it may take as much as twice the energy to start the car.

For a healthy battery with lots of chemicals left in it, there's usually no problem. However, for an older battery

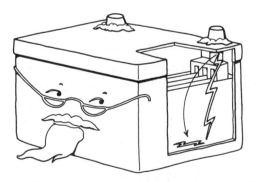

The white powdery substance that collects on the battery terminals eventually blocks electrical current.

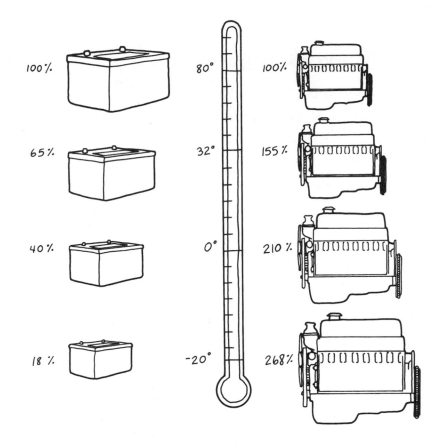

Battery's efficiency   Energy needed to start car

A battery's efficiency is dramatically affected by the temperature. On a very cold day, a battery may lose up to 80 percent of its ability to provide a spark, while it may take twice the energy to start the car.

❖

If you live in a cold climate, you may want to consider investing in an engine or battery heater, which can decrease the power needed to start a car.

that has used up a lot of its chemicals, losing 80 percent of its starting ability—when it didn't have too much to begin with—may be the last straw. Have your battery inspected during a pre-winter check, so it won't leave you in the lurch when the snow flies. If it needs to be replaced (see below for more about replacement), have it replaced then by someone you know and trust; don't wait until the freezing cold morning it fails to have it replaced by the tow-trucker who will probably only have one battery to sell you—the million-dollar brand.

Making your car go the distance
Ignition and Charging Systems

If all the systems and their component parts are in working order, a car is said to be tuned correctly. The sound you will hear as you turn the ignition key is "vrrooon-vrrooon," the muffled sound of many explosions and the mark of a smooth-running engine. If not, you may hear a lot of "rrreh-rrrehs" before you finally get a "vrrooon-vrrooon." If things are really fouled up, you may hear no sound at all. Following are important facts about the ignition and charging systems that can help make yours more reliable and trouble-free.

✓ Pay extra attention to your battery's maintenance if you live in a warm climate. Hot starts may require more battery power than cold starts so restarting problems can occur when the engine is hot.

✓ Don't make your starter work harder by turning the ignition key for more than 30 seconds; the excess heat will send it to an early grave. Allow cool-down periods between starting attempts.

✓ Before replacing a battery, have a competent technician inspect all ignition and charging components—they may be the real culprits when a car won't start.

✓ If you leave on the headlights or radio and wake to discover a dead battery, don't automatically assume you need a new one. The battery may only need to be recharged. And it must be fully recharged before it can be tested to determine if a new battery is needed.

✓ A **load tester** completes the examination of a fully charged battery. It demands that the battery provide the electrical current necessary to start the car under

A load tester

the simulated conditions of a cold day—the battery's toughest job. If the battery can't generate 9.6 volts at 0° F (-18° C) for 15 seconds it should be replaced.

✓ Periodically check the electrolyte level of a conventional battery by removing the plastic protective covers. The solution inside should reach the bottom of the plastic filler necks. If it doesn't, add distilled water. *Note:* While most batteries today are maintenance-free, it's a good idea to have it professionally tested once a year.

✓ Replace your battery with one of the same size and same (or higher) rating. Charts are available wherever batteries are sold to help you decide which size is right for your car. Do not buy a battery that is rated lower than your owner's manual recommends, or lower than the original battery.

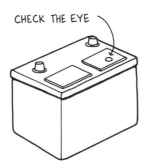

CHECK THE EYE

✓ If you have recently installed electronic accessories, such as a cellular telephone or an alarm system, consider upgrading to a higher-rated battery when it comes time to replace your old battery.

✓ When shopping for a new battery, consider the number of years you expect to keep your car. If

On maintenance-free batteries, you can peer at the built-in charge indicator, often called an "eye." If the eye is lit up, your battery is sufficiently charged; if it's dark, it must be charged before testing.

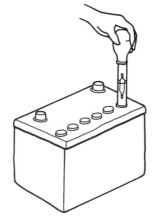

On a conventional battery, your service technician will use a hydrometer (a device that looks like a turkey baster) to determine the general health of the battery.

Money-Saving Tip

The cost of scheduled service varies depending on the tests, adjustments, and repairs that are needed; the make, model, and year of the car; and even the area of the country in which you live. Always call all a few places to be sure that the price you are quoted for service is fair. And be sure you know exactly what is included in each quote you get.

you're planning on selling your car in six months, think twice before buying a 60-month battery.

✓ Inspect the following starting, charging, and ignition components—as well as any others listed in your owner's manual—once a year, or whenever your owner's manual recommends. Fall, before the onset of cold weather, is a good time for the inspections.
- Inspect and clean battery terminals.
- Inspect battery cables and wires.
- Clean, adjust, or replace spark plugs as needed.
- Inspect distributor if applicable.
- Inspect belts for proper tension and replace brittle, flaky, or cracked belts.

✓ Advances in technology are to thank for some newer vehicles that do not require their first scheduled service for 100,000 miles (160,000 kilometers)! These vehicles still require fluid changes and periodic inspections. See your owner's manual for specifics.

Warning!
Do not smoke near a battery or expose it to an open flame of any kind. Batteries contain explosive gases.

Troubleshooting the Ignition and Charging Systems

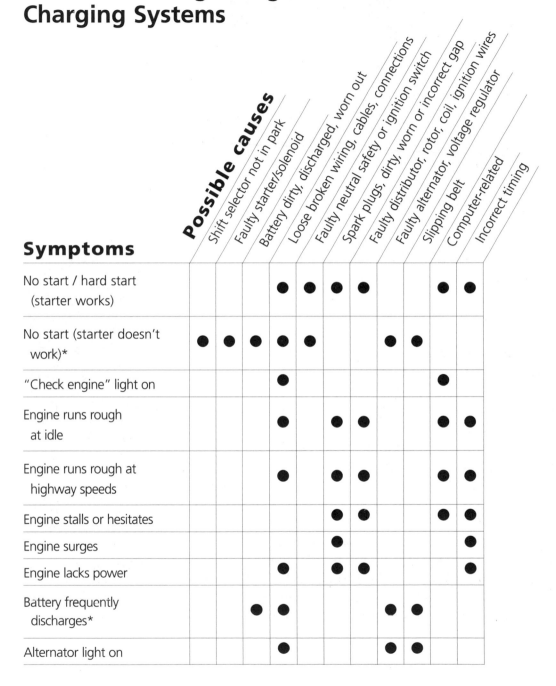

Possible causes

Symptoms	Shift selector not in park	Faulty starter/solenoid	Battery dirty, discharged, worn out	Loose broken wiring, cables, connections	Faulty neutral safety or ignition switch	Spark plugs, dirty, worn or incorrect gap	Faulty distributor, rotor, coil, ignition wires	Faulty alternator, voltage regulator	Slipping belt	Computer-related	Incorrect timing
No start / hard start (starter works)			●	●	●	●				●	●
No start (starter doesn't work)*	●	●	●	●	●			●	●		
"Check engine" light on			●							●	
Engine runs rough at idle			●			●	●			●	●
Engine runs rough at highway speeds			●			●	●			●	●
Engine stalls or hesitates						●	●			●	●
Engine surges						●					●
Engine lacks power			●			●	●				●
Battery frequently discharges*		●	●					●	●		
Alternator light on			●					●	●		

*Check battery terminals first. Dirt and/or corrosion are often the problem.

5
THE ENGINE

This chapter explains how the engine works and why it sometimes doesn't. It offers specific advice on how to maintain your car's engine, and, if repairs are necessary, what you can do to keep the repair bill somewhere below the national deficit and more in the range of a fast-food dinner for a family of four.

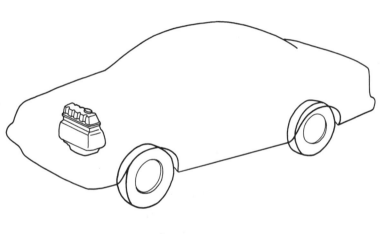

The engine
❖

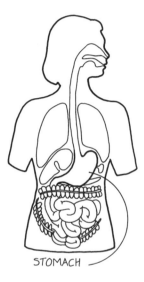

STOMACH

Think of the engine as your car's stomach. Just as your stomach transforms food into energy (with the help of digestive juices), so does your car's engine convert its diet of air and fuel into energy.

How the Engine Works

The engine takes the chemical energy available in its air-and-fuel diet and, with the help of the spark, converts it into the mechanical energy or motion of its pistons. This motion is then transferred through a series of metal rods to the wheels.

The expanded gases that result from the explosions would drive a piston right out the bottom of the engine

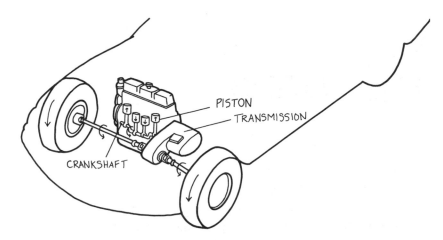

The energy of the pistons is transferred through a series of metal rods to the wheels.

❖

were it not firmly attached to the turning crankshaft. Good thing, too, or we'd be forever stopping to pick them up off the pavement, making progress slow and very expensive.

This impressive transfer of power is what cars are all about: the grand finale, the *pièce de résistance*, and so on.

Engine Layouts

All gasoline engines have certain things in common: Round metal plugs called pistons move up and down as a result of explosions that take place inside smooth round holes called cylinders, which are cut into a hunk of solid metal aptly named the **engine block**. Got that? Good. It's the basis for all knowledge about the engine.

Engines come in a variety of shapes and sizes. The three most common engine layouts as seen on the following page are 1) four or more cylinders "in-line" (in a row), attached to the crankshaft, 2) six cylinders in two rows of three, joined to the crankshaft in a V formation, and 3) eight cylinders arranged in two rows of four, also in V formation.

The heat of the internal explosions causes the pistons and cylinders to expand at different rates. If a piston were machined to the exact size of the cylinder, there wouldn't be enough room when it expanded for it to move at the breathtaking speed it does. Space must be provided to allow for the expansion, but space would allow gases to escape from the cylinders and reduce compression and power. What to do? Surround the piston by a thin metal ring that expands into the combustion chamber, sealing it and scraping excess oil from the cylinder walls. These rings permit movement, but keep gases from escaping because they act as a seal once the engine heats up.

Each piston is surrounded by thin metal rings that help to ensure compression and power by sealing in gases.

The Valves

Most of the valve train components are located in a separate metal casing placed over the engine block called the **engine head**. A thin piece of tough material, the **head gasket**, seals the opening where the engine block and head meet.

Located over the top of each cylinder, you will see two objects that look like upside-down golf tees—the **valves**. These valves are actually one-way doors, similar to the valves in your heart, which allow blood to flow in only one direction. Each cylinder has a minimum of two valves: an **intake valve** and an **exhaust valve**.

The intake valve opens to let the unburned fuel mixture into the upper area of the cylinders, the **combustion chamber**, where the air/fuel mixture will be burned. The valve closes tightly after the fuel mixture is admitted and

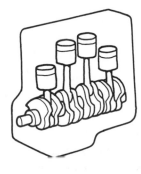

In-line 4 cylinder

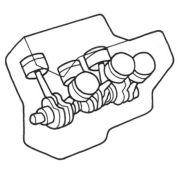

V-6 cylinder

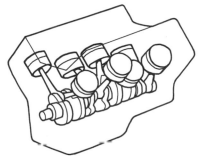

V-8 cylinder

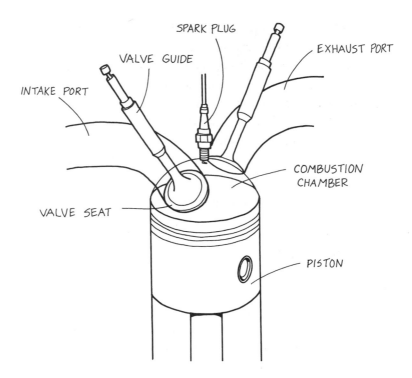

INTAKE PORT

VALVE GUIDE

SPARK PLUG

EXHAUST PORT

COMBUSTION CHAMBER

VALVE SEAT

PISTON

Valves in the engine act like the valves in your heart. They are one-way doors that regulate the flow of air and fuel into and out of the cylinders.

❖

while it is burning. The exhaust valve opens to permit the burned gases to exit after each burning, thus making room for a new air/fuel mixture to enter once again, via the intake valve.

The valves are attached to the **camshaft**, a round metal bar that gets its name from its metal bumps, or lobes, called **cams**. The camshaft is linked to the crankshaft by a **timing chain**, or **timing belt**. Because these two bars—the crankshaft and the camshaft—are attached to one another, when one turns, so does the other. As the camshaft turns, its lobes push against the valves, forcing them to open and close.

Valves never work solo. Depending on the specific design of the engine, hundreds of other parts, lumped under the heading **valve train**, help the valves open and close.

There are several different ways that valve trains can be designed. In a pushrod engine, the camshaft is positioned down in the engine block and connected to the valves by a series of components. These include **springs**, **rocker arms**, **pushrods**, and **tappets**. (An engine that has more than one camshaft—one for intake valves and one for exhaust valves—is called a **dual** or **double overhead cam** engine.)

Alternatively, the camshaft may sit directly over the valves. This popular design is referred to as an **overhead cam engine**. Since there are fewer parts connecting the camshaft to the valves, the engine can often run at higher speeds and produce more power than a similarly sized

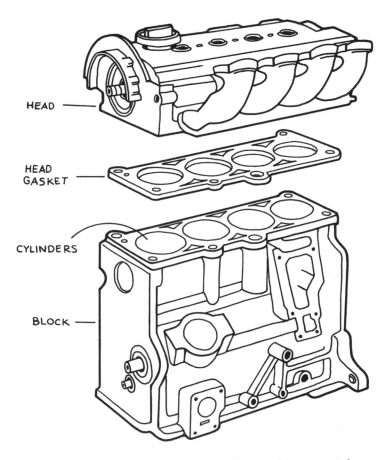

HEAD

HEAD GASKET

CYLINDERS

BLOCK

Most of the valve components are located in a metal casing called the head. A piece of tough material called the head gasket seals the two surfaces.

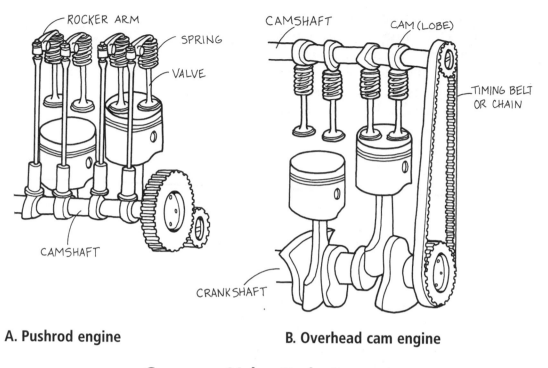

ROCKER ARM
SPRING
VALVE
CAMSHAFT

CAMSHAFT
CAM (LOBE)
TIMING BELT
OR CHAIN
CRANKSHAFT

A. Pushrod engine   **B. Overhead cam engine**

Common Valve Train Layouts

❖

pushrod engine. With either design, smooth engine performance depends on many small but important parts working in harmony with each other.

The Four Strokes of an Engine

Each movement of a piston, up or down, is called a **stroke**. It takes four strokes to produce power. Let's track the path of just one piston, piston number two, as it plays its part. Each of the other pistons will be doing the same thing, but at a different time.

On stroke 1, the **intake stroke**, the piston moves downward because it is attached to the crankshaft. On cue, the intake valve begins to open. The piston now acts like a big straw drawing the air/fuel mixture in behind it. *Whoosh.* When the cylinder is filled with vapor, the valve closes. The combustion chamber is now sealed.

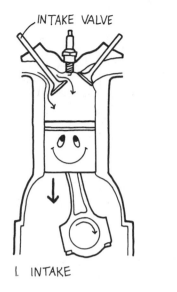

1. INTAKE

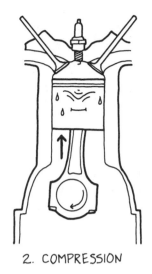

2. COMPRESSION

The Four Strokes of an Engine

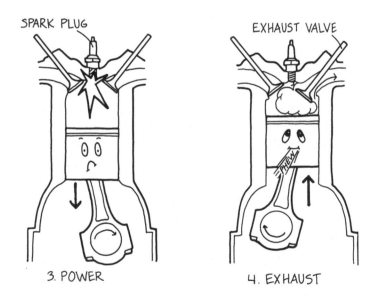

3. POWER

4. EXHAUST

On stroke 2, the **compression stroke**, the piston moves back up and compresses the fuel mixture into a small space at the top.

On stroke 3, the **power stroke**, the spark is delivered. The compressed air/fuel mixture explodes with the force

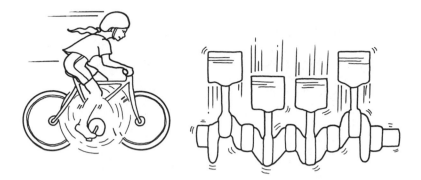

To return to the analogy of the bicyclist to the pistons: those legs just went from a smooth, slow pedal to a blur!

❖

of many sticks of dynamite—*Kablam!* The heated gases that result from the explosion expand and push the piston down violently.

During stroke 4, the **exhaust stroke**, which takes place after the explosion, the piston once again rises (this time because the piston next door has just fired, causing the crankshaft to turn again), and another valve, an exhaust valve, opens to expel the hot used gases.

The piston now acts like a reusable bullet. Its powerful and violent up-and-down motion happens over and over again—as many as 100 times per second! Within a fraction of a second, all the pistons are going up and down at the same amazing speed, but at different times, to reduce the vibration that would occur if they were all to ignite at once. The valves may open and close 100,000 times in an hour!

It takes four movements of the piston to turn the crankshaft two revolutions. The crankshaft must turn at a minimum number of revolutions per minute (rpms) to continue the self-perpetuating motion responsible for producing the turning power of the engine, or **torque**; otherwise, the engine would stall.

Timing

Fred Astaire and Ginger Rogers had it. All successful dancers have it. So do engines that run well. *Timing* is coordination. It is more than one person or part acting in unison to create a desired result.

To accomplish this model of performance, correct timing or coordination must take place among the hundreds of engine components that create, combine, compress, and explode the engine's air/fuel/spark diet. Each component acts like a dancer in a chorus line. If one dancer is a second late in the execution of a step, the entire performance will suffer, and the audience will not be pleased. In a chorus line, everyone must work together for a smooth effect.

The same is true for your car's engine. All the components must work together if the performance is to be smooth and error-free. That your engine—a conglomeration of hundreds of moving parts—performs as smoothly as it does most of the time is perhaps more surprising than that it occasionally stumbles.

It is timing that coordinates this mass of movement among the engine's numerous parts, thus ensuring maximum **compression**, which results in maximum engine power and fuel efficiency. The intake valve should open so that a maximum amount of the unburned air/fuel mixture reaches the combustion chamber before compression takes place. The exhaust valve should then open so that a maximum amount of burned gases leaves the chamber immediately after ignition takes place.

As Fred and Ginger knew, the key to a flawless performance is timing.

The spark reaches the spark plug at the correct moment—just before the piston reaches the top of the cylinder, having thoroughly compressed the air/fuel mixture. That moment in time is called **"Top Dead Center"** in garage-ese.

If the spark plug ignites the air/fuel mixture at any other time (for example, when the piston has already begun to descend), the piston will not travel as far and the engine will not produce as much power. Power is also lost if the valves open at the incorrect time; for example, during the power stroke.

Frequently asked questions

Q What is the difference between a diesel and a gasoline engine?

A The **diesel engine** is similar in many ways to a **gasoline engine** except that the fuel is ignited simply by the heat of the compressed air, not by a spark plug. Compressing air makes it hotter. In diesel engines, the air is compressed so tightly that it becomes red-hot. Fuel is injected into the cylinder by fuel injectors, then compressed, and the super hot air causes it to explode. What happens to the pistons after that is similar to what happens in gasoline engines. Diesel engines are traditionally more fuel-efficient than their gasoline cousins and able to operate on less expensive diesel fuel. The trade-offs are a heavier engine and a distinct intolerance for even small amounts of water in the fuel delivery system.

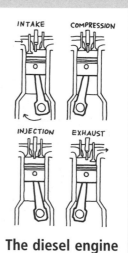

The diesel engine

The Computer

On today's cars, the on-board computer that is in charge of fuel delivery and ignition also controls timing and combustion. The computer analyzes the information it receives from many different sensors about the delivery of the spark, the movement of the crankshaft, and the opening and closing of the valves. It continually readjusts their activity for maximum power and efficiency.

The automotive computer controls timing and combustion.

The Power Play

Designing engines that produce more power while maintaining good fuel economy has always been one of automotive engineering's primary goals. Simply enlarging the combustion chambers of most small engines (increasing their **displacement**) provides more power, but it often increases the engine's vibration and sacrifices fuel economy. A desirable alternative is to keep the cylinder the same size and enable it to "eat" its air/fuel diet more quickly. Among the ways to accomplish this are adding valves, **superchargers**, or **turbochargers**.

Multi-valve Engines

Multi-valve engines are those with more than two valves per cylinder. The more air and fuel that enters the cylinders, the greater the explosion. The result is more power without sacrificing good gas economy. The advantages, however, are most noticeable when you accelerate hard, and less noticeable at slower speeds.

Superchargers and Turbochargers

Most engines are **normally aspirated**, that is, they draw the air/fuel mixture into the combustion chambers without

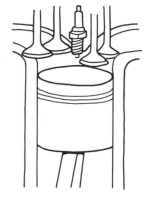

Multi-valve engines allow more air into the cylinders.

Money-Saving Tip

Have your timing belt or chain inspected and changed whenever your manufacturer recommends. If a timing belt breaks, it can act like a grenade inside an engine. In seconds it can severely damage valves and even pistons, resulting in expensive repairs to remedy the damage.

assistance. As the piston moves downward in the chamber, it creates a **vacuum** behind it into which the air/fuel mixture is drawn. It works like a big straw. To get more power out of a normally aspirated engine, it is necessary to force it to breathe more air and burn more fuel.

Superchargers and turbochargers are pumps that force more air and fuel into the combustion chambers of an engine, forcing them to burn more fuel and produce more power. A supercharger differs from a turbocharger primarily in the method it uses to get additional air and fuel into the combustion chambers.

A supercharger is driven by a belt, which works off the power of the engine. Consequently, it uses some power to provide other power.

Instead of a belt, a turbocharger uses a device called a **turbine**. A turbine is a machine with two sets of blades which spin in oil. The pump is placed in the path of the exhaust gases. Those hot gases turn one blade of the turbine, and that turns the other blade. This forces some of the exhaust gases back into the engine. Some of the heat that would normally go out the tailpipe as total waste is now used to generate additional power. Because it takes

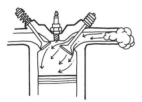

Superchargers and turbochargers force more air into the cylinders.

a second for the exhaust gases to be burned, there is a short delay, called a *lag*, in getting the extra boost to the engine.

Intercoolers and Tuned Intake Manifolds

Superchargers and turbochargers can produce even more power when they are equipped with an **intercooler**. This device, as its name suggests, cools air. Cooler air molecules allow more air molecules to be packed into the

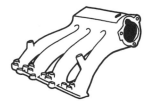

A tuned intake manifold makes an engine supercharger or turbocharger even more powerful.

Frequently asked questions

Q What can happen when a car's engine overheats?

A Your engine generates enough heat to melt ordinary steel. If too much heat accumulates, it will damage the engine. The heat can be so intense that it warps or twists the metal cylinder head. It may also burn away the layer of insulation called the head gasket, located between the head and the block. A warped or cracked cylinder head or a blown head gasket will permit the hot combustion gases to escape, resulting in a lack of power and potentially serious engine damage. As if that weren't enough, internal parts, such as pistons and their connecting rods, can warp or break. Even the engine block can crack. Or the worst possible case? The engine can seize—the pistons actually melt into the cylinder walls—never to move again.

Note: If your engine does overheat, turn the heater and the fan on high to help dissipate the heat. If that doesn't help, get the car safely off the road, turn the engine off, and let it cool down.

combustion chamber and burned for more power. A properly designed intercooler can increase power by 10 percent.

Another way of adding power is to redesign the steel tubes that carry the air/fuel mixture to and from the engine (the **intake manifold**) and the exhaust gases away from it (the **exhaust manifold**). Redesigning the manifolds makes the cylinder available for a fresh air/fuel mixture quicker. Both of these methods increase the engine's efficiency and generate more power.

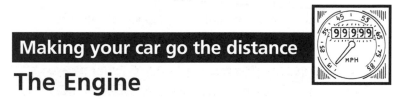

Making your car go the distance

The Engine

Following the schedule of service in your owner's manual will help keep your engine in good working order. Here are some other tips to make your engine last.

✓ Oil changes are the most important and should be the most frequently performed preventive maintenance. More than anything else you do for your vehicle, regularly changing the oil will extend the serviceable life of your engine. (See chapter 9 for more about oil.)

✓ Always give your vehicle a minute or two to warm up before driving off. It takes that long for the oil to reach and separate the hundreds of finely machined parts inside the engine.

✓ Before any internal engine work is done, make sure that the fuel and ignition systems have been inspected and adjusted to manufacturer's specifications. Internal engine repair is labor intensive and extremely expensive, so get a written estimate before okaying work. You may also want a second opinion.

✓   If any portion of your engine needs to be rebuilt, be
    sure the repair shop uses factory-rebuilt and war-
ranted equipment for the replacement parts.

✓   Valves, **valve guides** and seats, rings, and other
    internal parts wear over time, resulting in a loss of
power and an increase in oil consumption. You may have
to replace worn internal parts with new ones.

Troubleshooting the Engine

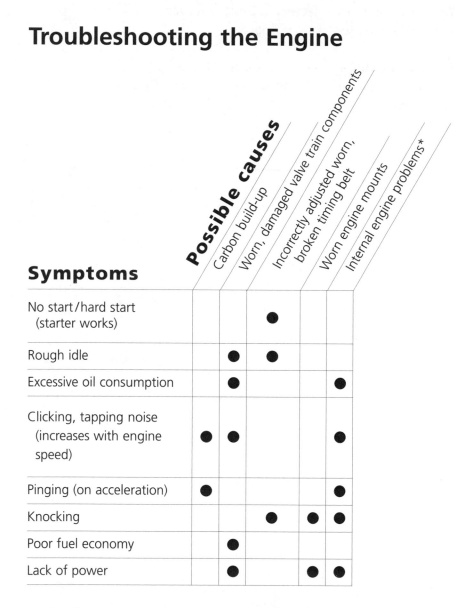

Symptoms	Carbon build-up	Worn, damaged valve train components	Incorrectly adjusted worn, broken timing belt	Worn engine mounts	Internal engine problems*
No start/hard start (starter works)			●		
Rough idle		●	●		
Excessive oil consumption		●			●
Clicking, tapping noise (increases with engine speed)	●	●			●
Pinging (on acceleration)	●				●
Knocking			●	●	●
Poor fuel economy		●			
Lack of power		●		●	●

*Before beginning internal engine diagnosis and repair, a technician should thoroughly inspect ignition, fuel, emission controls, and computerized elements.

6
THE EXHAUST SYSTEM AND EMISSION CONTROLS

Proper maintenance of the exhaust and emissions systems is important for the environment, as well as for your safety. This chapter explains how the exhaust and emission control systems work and how you can save money by taking advantage of a special warranty, should you need repairs to these systems.

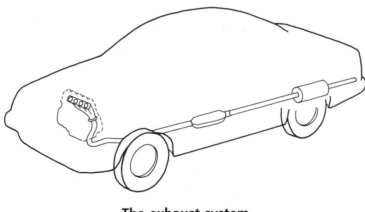

The exhaust system
❖

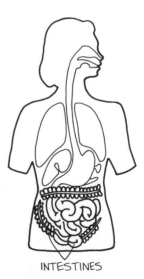

INTESTINES

The exhaust system and emission controls are analogous to the human body's intestines.

Like the human body, cars generate waste, and they must have a way to remove those waste products from their systems in order to remain healthy. The **exhaust system** and emission controls are analogous to the body's intestines. They draw the waste products of combustion, hot exhaust gases, away from the engine and into the atmosphere.

These automobile waste products contribute to air pollution. The primary offenders are hydrocarbons, nitrogen oxides, and carbon monoxide. Hydrocarbons and nitrogen oxides are visible in the form of brown clouds that hang over many of our cities—smog. Carbon monoxide, while invisible, is believed to be partly responsible for the attack on the earth's ozone layer.

How the Exhaust System Works

The exhaust system begins at the exhaust manifold, a set of steel pipes that are attached to the engine. Combustion gases that have escaped through the exhaust valves collect in the manifold after burning. These gases are pushed along by the pressure of the incoming gases, until they flow into one or more steel pipes, the **headpipes**.

From the headpipe, the gases go to the **catalytic converter**, a device that looks like a large muffler and contains precious metals that cause a chemical reaction. These metals turn carbon monoxide and hydrocarbons into harmless substances such as water and carbon dioxide.

From the converter, gases go on to the **muffler**, an oblong metal noise-catcher that absorbs much of the sound that combustion creates by routing sound waves

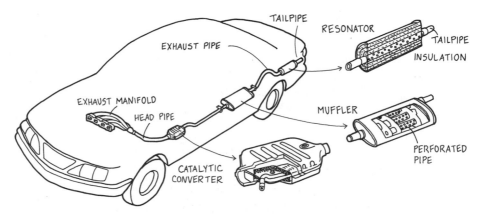

The exhaust system is made up of a series of metal components that are welded together to route burned gases away from the engine and into the atmosphere.

Frequently asked questions

Q Why does my car smell like rotten eggs?

A The catalytic converter is often responsible for this odor. It occurs as a result of the burning of sulfur present in gasoline. It's normal for this odor to occur occasionally, but it can be a warning sign of a clogged or defective system. Try switching brands of gasoline. If that doesn't help, check with your dealer to see if there is a factory fix, and ask if the cost is covered by warranty.

through its perforated pipes. The remaining gases may reach the atmosphere by way of the final exhaust pipe, the **tailpipe**, or they may pass through another sound-reducing device called a **resonator**. What reaches the atmosphere is our car's contribution to the planet: pollution.

The Emission Control System

Since the early 1960s, environmental protection laws have attempted to reduce pollutants by requiring the use of certain exhaust and emission control devices that control the amount of pollutants (gases and particulates) engines produce. To describe in depth the emission control components found on most cars today, we would need another book of this size. What is important to know is that emission control components are instrumental in reducing pollution. Unfortunately, they also affect the performance of your car's engine.

Here is a list of some of the major devices and a brief description of how they work. (Your car may have a few or many of these emission control devices, as well as additional devices not listed here.)

The **exhaust gas recirculation (EGR) system** recirculates exhaust gases back to the engine, where they are burned again.

Warning!

A faulty exhaust system can allow harmful gases into the passenger compartment, resulting in possible carbon monoxide poisoning. An annual inspection by a service professional is a must.

Many states require vehicles to pass an emissions standards test before new tags will be issued.

❖

The **exhaust gas conversion** system includes the catalytic converter and *oxygen sensor*.

The **evaporative emission control (EEC) system** traps vapors from the fuel system and redirects them to the engine, where they are stored in a charcoal canister. Instead of being released into the atmosphere, these fumes are burned in the engine when the engine is restarted.

The **positive crankcase ventilation (PCV) system** picks up "blow-by gases" that have escaped into the crankcase from the combustion chambers and returns them to the engine to be burned.

The **pre-heated-air-intake system** uses hot exhaust gases to maintain the flow of warm air into the engine.

Money-Saving Tip

Special Federal Emissions Warranty

If your emission control system fails because of a defective part, whether or not the part failure causes your car's emissions to exceed federal emission standards, the manufacturer is required by federal law to pay for the repairs for the first five years or 50,000 miles (80,000 kilometers).

This allows for a more combustible mixture that requires less fuel and burns more completely.

Many of the ignition and fuel delivery components on both fuel-injected and carburetor models have been developed to control emissions. On fuel-injected systems, these devices include the fuel injectors and the computer. On carburetor models, the mixture control unit, the electronic choke, and the thermostatic air cleaner were developed to help curb emissions.

Often, retightening exhaust components will remedy rattles in the system.

Making your car go the distance
Exhaust and Emission Control Systems

The exhaust and emissions systems should be checked regularly to ensure that they are operating correctly. Here are some other items to be aware of.

✓ Rattles, roars, knocks, buzzes, and chatters coming from under the car, particularly those that are especially noticeable at idle, are very often the result of loose parts, fasteners, or hangers. Many times, simply retightening the exhaust components will set the system right.

✓ If your muffler needs replacement and you are told that it is a one-piece assembly (meaning you must buy the exhaust pipe as well as the muffler, even though your exhaust pipe might be in good shape), ask if there is an adapter that will allow the new muffler to be fitted to your old exhaust pipe.

✓ Always read the guarantee for muffler replacement carefully, and file it and the bill in a safe place.

✓ In many places government regulations require vehicles to pass an emission standards test. Having your vehicle serviced regularly will help it to pass even the most rigorous local inspection programs.

Troubleshooting the Exhaust System and Emission Controls

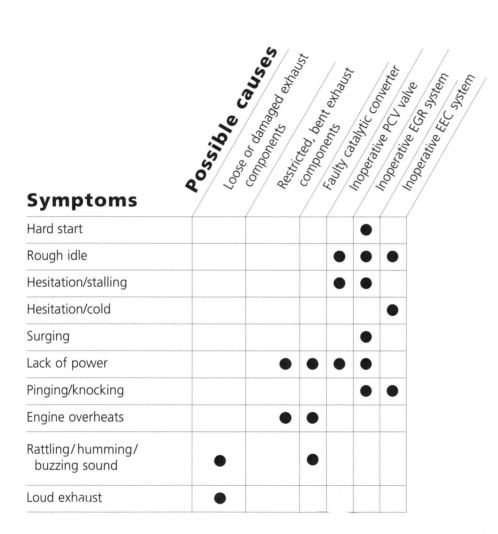

Symptoms	**Possible causes** Loose or damaged exhaust components	Restricted, bent exhaust components	Faulty catalytic converter	Inoperative PCV valve	Inoperative EGR system	Inoperative EEC system
Hard start				●		
Rough idle			●	●	●	
Hesitation/stalling			●	●		
Hesitation/cold						●
Surging				●		
Lack of power		●	●	●	●	
Pinging/knocking					●	●
Engine overheats		●	●			
Rattling/humming/ buzzing sound	●		●			
Loud exhaust	●					

7
THE ELECTRICAL SYSTEM

Without the electrical network, your vehicle's "nervous system," none of the car's other systems can function. In this chapter, you'll learn why electrical problems occur, and how to handle the simpler repairs while avoiding paying too much for the not-so-simple repairs.

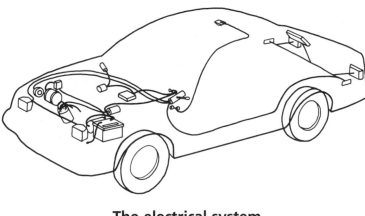

The electrical system
❖

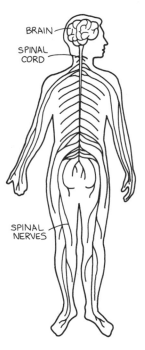

BRAIN
SPINAL CORD
SPINAL NERVES

Your car's electrical system can be compared to the human body's nervous system.

The electrical system of your car acts like the nervous system in your body. In your body, important messages are passed through nerve cells in the form of tiny electrical currents. In your car, messages are passed through metal wires in the form of not-so-tiny electrical currents. Automotive messages are converted into power for the ignition, computers, lights, and accessories.

Just as the body has more than one nervous system—one for the muscles and another that controls such functions as sweating—so, too, do cars. Today's cars have at

least two electrical systems, sometimes more. The central electrical system controls the ignition, lights, and accessories, while a second system controls the engine management computer. There may also be a third system, one to control such devices as electronic brakes. For more about brakes, see chapter 13.

How the Electrical System Works

Electricity begins and ends at the battery. That's where electrical current rests when the engine is not running. When the engine is turned on, current leaves the battery to provide electricity for the ignition, lights, and accessories. Electrical currents, though, are essentially homebodies; they will not leave the battery unless they are assured of a return ticket home. In electrical terms, that return ticket is called a **circuit**, or return loop.

It's the same in your home. Current will not flow without a return loop. In your home, a metal wire takes the current to its destination and returns it to its point of origin by way of a second metal wire. With lots of storage space hidden behind the walls of your home, this system works great. In your car, a wiring system that provided a second return wire for each light and accessory would look like a spaghetti factory gone berserk. Your car's frame, being made of metal, makes a great oversized return wire. It is the frame of the car that pro-

Electrical current will not flow unless there is a return loop.

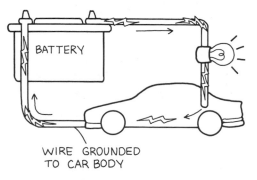

WIRE GROUNDED
TO CAR BODY

The metal frame of the car acts as an oversized return wire and provides the return loop for electrical current. This is referred to as grounding.

vides the return loop for the electrical current and completes the circuit. This is referred to as **grounding**. Any cable, strap, metal bolt, or mount that connects an electrical component to the frame is called a ground.

Switches, Relays, Fuses, Fusible Links, and Circuit Breakers

Each return loop or circuit has a **switch** that acts like a drawbridge. When the drawbridge is lowered, the circuit is complete and the current can move or flow; when the drawbridge is up, the circuit is incomplete and the current cannot flow. For example, when you turn on the headlights for night driving, a switch lowers the drawbridge for that light's circuit, the circuit is complete, and current flows to the headlights.

Relays are backup safety switches that are used on circuits with particularly strong electrical current; for example, the ignition, the windshield wiper motor, and the horn.

Just as any metal or plastic device can malfunction, so can switches and relays. A relay can simply stop working, and current will not flow to the accessory in its charge. A switch can become stuck in the "on" position, completing the circuit so there is current constantly going to the light

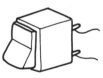

SWITCH

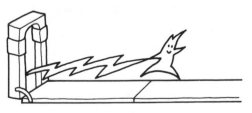

Switches and relays act like drawbridges: they allow electrical current to move across them only when they're lowered.

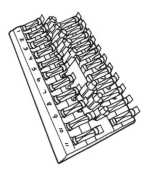

Consult your owner's manual for the location of the fuse boxes in your car.

or accessory—even when you assume it's not. Even if the accessory or light doesn't use a lot of current, it doesn't take long before the reserve current of the battery is completely used up—and you have a dead battery on your hands. *Note:* Recharging the battery and replacing the switch will usually solve the problem.

Fuses, fusible links, and circuit breakers guard the electrical system from fires resulting from overheating due to excessive electricity. Most accessories have fuses that are wires contained within plastic or glass tubes. If too much voltage surges through a circuit and causes it to get too hot, the wire element in the fuse melts or "blows." Consequently, there is a gap of air between the wires that carry the current. Air is an insulator, not a conductor of current; it prevents the passage of electricity. So when a fuse blows, the flow of current is interrupted.

Fusible links accomplish the same thing as fuses, but rather than being enclosed in glass or plastic and placed together in a box, they are thinner pieces of wire located at strategic points in the wiring. If there is a surge of current, the thinner wire melts and the circuit is broken.

Circuit breakers are spring-loaded devices that retract

Money-Saving Tip

Whenever there is a problem anywhere in your car's electrical system, check first to see if there is a fuse for that accessory. If there is, examine it to see whether it is blown—the fuse's metal strip is broken or blackened—before you send for help. It is an all-too-common occurrence today for cars to be towed into dealerships and service stations when the problem could have been remedied with an inexpensive fuse. Don't waste your time and money.

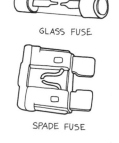

GLASS FUSE

SPADE FUSE

The solution to an electrical problem may be as simple as replacing a blown fuse.

when they receive a current surge. To be without the use of an accessory because a fuse, fusible link, or circuit breaker has melted or sprung may be very inconvenient temporarily, but it sure beats the alternative—a fire.

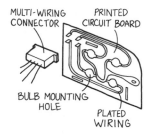

Printed circuits of metal bonded onto plastic are often used behind the dashboard to reduce the amount of wiring.

Warning! If you detect the odor of burning rubber or plastic while driving, it could be the wiring insulation burning away from, or rubbing against, the metal of the body. This is a warning to be heeded! Have the electrical system inspected as soon as possible. It could be the start of an electrical fire.

What Can Go Wrong?

Electrical problems invariably result from the inability of electrical current to get from the battery to the component and back to the battery again. This inability to return home is usually the result of a **short** or an **open**.

A short is a circuit that is accidentally shortened; it forces the current to return to its source before it reaches its destination (a headlight, for example, or the horn). A short often is the result of the insulating material around the wire wearing away. Stripped of its insulation, the wire can touch against the metal of the car, and the current can return home via the quickest and easiest path, the frame.

A short often causes a fuse to blow. If a fuse is replaced and it blows again immediately, it could be that the vibration of the car traveling along the road is causing the intermittent contact of a wire with the car's metal frame. If it happens often and can't be traced, the only answer is to replace the wiring in that circuit.

An open circuit can also cause the flow of current to be interrupted. If a wire is broken or frayed in such a way that air comes between the two pieces of wire, the air acts as an insulator, not a conductor, and interrupts the flow of current. An open circuit can occur as a result of a broken wire, a bad switch, a burned-out bulb, a malfunctioning motor, or a faulty connection. One of the most common

A short is a circuit that returns to the battery before reaching its destination.

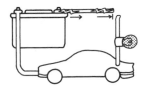

One of the most common opens occurs when dirt restricts the movement of current where two wires meet.

Starting, Charging, and Ignition Circuits

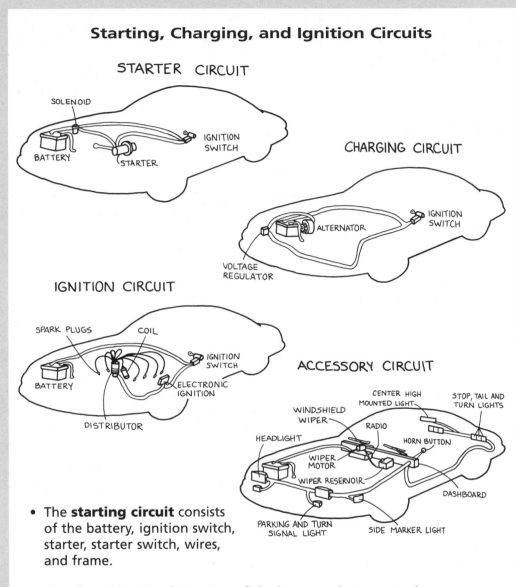

- The **starting circuit** consists of the battery, ignition switch, starter, starter switch, wires, and frame.

- The **charging circuit** consists of the battery, alternator, voltage regulator, wires, and frame.

- The **ignition circuit** consists of the battery, ignition switch, coil, distributor, spark plugs, and computer.

- The **accessory circuit** consists of the battery, lights, dash instruments, windshield wiper, horn, and any other power devices, including seats, windows, or antenna.

opens occurs when dirt or corrosion collects where two wires connect. The dirt creates resistance and restricts the movement of the current. Cleaning or replacing the connector should correct the problem.

Lights

The light system includes brake lights, headlights, side markers, directional lights, and hazard lights, which are all mandatory on today's cars. Most lights operate in a similar manner: wires run through and into a bulb that is attached to a tungsten filament, a piece of fine wire. Current flows to the bulb through the wire and the socket, and then on to the filament. The current causes tiny particles in the filament to heat up, sending out showers of glowing sparks. This glow is called incandescence. A bulb can contain more than one filament, as do taillights, stoplights, and some headlights.

Dashboard Instrumentation

The instrumentation circuit is made up of gauges and warning lights. A **sending unit** or sensor relays

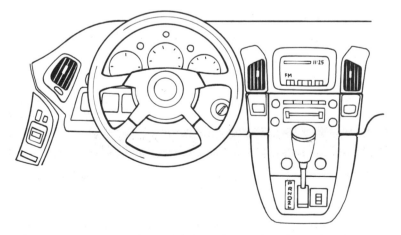

When you turn on the vehicle, all the dashboard lights should go on, then go out immediately. See your owner's manual for specifics.

Worn, cracked, or dirty windshield wiper blades can be a real safety hazard.

information to the gauges or computer about the volume, temperature, and pressure of the gasoline, oil, and coolant, among other things.

Turn Signals

Today's directionals are operated by a **flasher unit**. That's a switch that turns the directional bulbs on and off 60 to 120 times per minute; it also activates the flashing emergency hazard lights.

Windshield Wipers

The windshield wipers are run by a small electrical motor that has a connecting arm to the wiper arms. Wiper motors have a fuse and at least one, and sometimes two, switches. The first switch signals the wipers to stop, while the second switch, called the wiper park switch, allows the wiper arms to return to their original position after you turn them off.

The Horn

Depressing the horn button sends an electrical current to a magnet, causing a vibration that results in an audible signal.

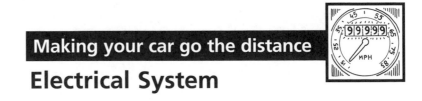

Making your car go the distance

Electrical System

Modern wiring systems, despite their complexity, cause relatively few problems and usually require little attention. Here are a few tips to keep the system operating smoothly.

✔ Inspect all of your car's lights, directionals, and warning signals monthly to be sure they are working properly. Check your owner's manual for the correct procedure for changing the bulbs in your car.

✔ Make sure your car's horn is working correctly by giving it a blast on a regular basis.

✔ Inspect windshield wiper blades whenever you clean your windshield. Replace blades at least once a year or when they become cracked or brittle, or smear the windshield.

✔ If you live in an area with severe winters, switch to winter blades before the season's first snowfall. And be sure to clean off heavy deposits of snow and free frozen or stuck wiper blades before turning on the car.

✔ If your windshield wipers stop working, it could be just a blown fuse, not a failed motor. Before the motor is replaced, be sure the fuse is okay.

✔ All cars have at least one fuse box, and many have more than one. To find the fuse box in your car, look in your owner's manual or have your service provider show you.

✔ Be sure you carry extra fuses that are the correct size as indicated in your owner's manual.

✔ Get in the habit of turning off all electrical devices when you park the car.

Warning!

Touching a halogen bulb—such as those used in headlights—with your bare hands will destroy it. Always wear gloves.

Troubleshooting the Electrical System

Possible causes

Symptoms	Faulty switch	Battery discharged, worn out	Bulb, contact at bulb socket	Fuse*	Fusible link, circuit breaker switch relay	Wiring, ground, connection	Voltage regulator	Instrument voltage regulator	Gauge, sending unit sensor	Flasher unit, turn signal
Headlights dim	●	●	●			●	●			
Headlights don't work	●		●	●	●	●				
No high or low beam	●		●	●		●				
Bulbs burn out frequently							●			
Turn signals don't work	●			●		●				●
Turn signals flash on one side only	●		●	●		●				
Warning lights or gauges don't work			●			●		●	●	
Power windows or locks don't work	●			●	●	●				
Horn doesn't work					●	●				
Windshield wipers don't work	●			●		●				

*Always check fuses first when troubleshooting any electrical problem.

8
AUTOMOTIVE COMPUTERS

Most cars built today have at least one, and usually several, on-board computers. This chapter explains how automotive computers work and why they have changed the nature and cost of auto repairs. You'll learn what you can do to minimize repair costs and what to do if you have an intermittent performance problem.

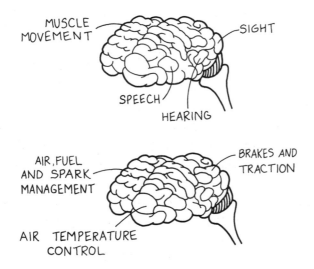

The automotive computer is the car's "brain." Just as different parts of the brain do different jobs, different parts of the computer serve different functions.

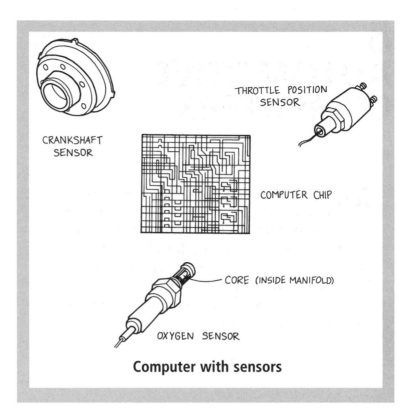

CRANKSHAFT SENSOR

THROTTLE POSITION SENSOR

COMPUTER CHIP

CORE (INSIDE MANIFOLD)

OXYGEN SENSOR

Computer with sensors

TOUCH

COLD

WARMTH

PRESSURE

PAIN

SKIN RECEPTORS

The brain and the computer both receive information from different types of receptors.

The computer in your car, sometimes called an electronic control module (ECM) or electronic control unit (ECU), is really a computer chip or microprocessor. Similar to the central processing unit in your personal computer, it's an on-board, whiz-bang electronic brain. And like all brains, it processes information and comes up with answers, making possible the successful completion of many tasks.

Just as different parts of the human brain do different jobs, different parts of the computer serve different functions. The cerebrum controls memory and thinking, for example, and the cerebellum controls the nerves. In a car's "brain," one part controls fuel management and delivery while another is in charge of spark control.

Not only that, your car probably has more than one computer—perhaps as many as three or more. One computer is in charge of engine management, one may control the temperature inside the passenger compartment, and another may be helping you to avoid skids by controlling the brakes and traction.

The human brain and automotive computer both receive information from different types of receptors. The body's receptors give us our senses—taste, smell, and the ability to feel pain, for example. The car's "receptors" are electronic sensors or feelers that record information about the speed of the engine (the engine rpm sensor), the temperature of the coolant (coolant sensor), the position of the accelerator pedal (throttle position sensor), and many other factors. This information helps the car to run smoothly and efficiently.

How Computers Work

In order to function properly, your brain relies on the information it receives from your sense organs. Different types of receptors record information about the things you come in contact with in your world. Your skin, for example, has millions of nerve endings that act as pain receptors. If you eat a piece of pizza that is too hot, a pain signal is sent to the brain that says "Ouch! Do something to protect yourself from being burned!"

The automotive equivalent of the body's receptors are sensors—electronic eyes, ears, and nerve endings that record information about the speed of the engine, the temperature and density of the outside air, and much more. With this input, the computer then determines the

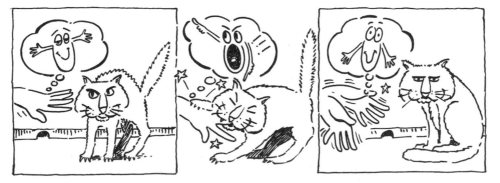

How receptors work in humans: Person pets cat with a bad attitude; pain receptors inside the "petter" send signals to direct the muscles to withdraw the hand from the "petee." This solves the problem by taking away the source of the pain.

best air/fuel mixture, how hot the spark should be, and when it should be delivered, what to do to reduce emissions, and hundreds of other pieces of information that help the car to run smoothly and efficiently.

The car's computer works in a similar way. Among the engine computer's sensors is an oxygen sensor, referred to in the automobile industry as the "O_2 sensor." This important device monitors the amount of oxygen left in the stream of exhaust gases leaving the engine. If the O_2 sensor finds that the mixture has too much or too little oxygen, it informs the computer in the form of light-ning-fast Morse code. If the computer detects too much oxygen, for example, it consults a database where alternative air/fuel combinations ideally suited for different driving conditions are stored. Like all computer information, these combinations are stored in memory boxes called cells. Having found the right cell, the computer corrects the air/fuel mixture by instructing the fuel injectors that more fuel is needed. It changes the length of time that the injectors remain open or turns them on more frequently, thus changing the amount of fuel delivered.

A computer may fine-tune the air/fuel mixture as many as ten times a second! That's child's play for this brain, since its electronic signals are traveling at the speed of light: 186,000 miles (299,500 kilometers) per second!

There are, however, limits to the electronic problem-

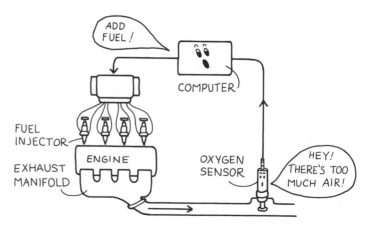

The oxygen sensor monitors the amount of oxygen left in the stream of exhaust gases leaving the engine.

When automotive sensors don't work, the driver usually notices engine performance problems.

❖

solving system. Just as with your body, if one or more of your senses were to malfunction, you'd have difficulty operating normally. Likewise, trouble occurs when automotive sensors are damaged by dirt, excessive heat, or vibrations. This can garble the data sent to the computer, or cut it off completely. When this occurs, the driver usually notices engine performance problems, such as hard starting, rough running, power loss, and even stalling. Poor fuel economy and high emissions may also be the result of sensor malfunction. When problems such as these crop up, it's time for a professional to analyze the system.

When Things Go Wrong

Computer care is a job for the experts. Just as you wouldn't want anyone but a trained neurosurgeon to

Computers are improving the efficiency and safety of our vehicles. Some computers act as radars, warning us to take evasive action if another object gets too close for comfort. Still others can map out the best route to take with the fewest traffic tie-ups.

Although it's not exactly wizardry, computer care is definitely a job for the experts.

❖

operate on your brain, you shouldn't want anyone but a trained technician to care for your car's brain. A medical doctor can often diagnose a patient's problems by listening to her symptoms and then running a series of specific tests based on those symptoms. In the same way, a service technician with the proper training and test equipment can track down a car's problems and correct them.

Automotive computers monitor their own activity. When a problem is detected, the computer often stores the problem as a number, a "trouble code," in its memory. By connecting an engine analyzer to the on-board computer, a technician can draw data from the analyzer, diagnose the problem, and suggest the most likely causes. The technician may then make a precise adjustment or replace a faulty sensor or other computer component. When the check is run again, the code displayed will indicate that the problem has been corrected, or, if not, the test will be run again and the next likely set of causes reviewed.

Intermittent Problems

But what happens if the problem did not register a trouble code and will not duplicate itself for the benefit of the technician? Just as our teeth seem to stop aching whenever we sit down in the dentist's chair, a car often seems to get better the closer we get to the repair shop. Naturally, if it is an intermittent problem, you will want the technician to road test the car in order to re-create the problem, but even that may not help if the car is unwilling to cooperate.

Fortunately, some computers do record intermittent problems. For those that don't, there is equipment available, similar to an airplane's flight recorder, that can be installed on an uncooperative vehicle to detect a sporadic problem. The car can be driven normally until the problem occurs again, when the device will register it. Unfortunately, these devices (sometimes referred to as "flight recorders" by technicians) are expensive. They will, however, capture that elusive intermittent problem and record it so that the culprit can be identified and remedied. If you are experiencing this type of problem, ask if the shop you are working with has this device. If not, find one that

Money-Saving Tip

If you are told that your car's computer or one of its sensors is defective, be sure you work with a dealership. In most cases the computer is covered under the manufacturer's warranty, or under the 5-year, 50,000-miles federal emission warranty.

Diagnostic devices are available which can be installed in a vehicle to detect intermittent problems.

Just as you would with a doctor, get a second opinion if the cause of your problem is not diagnosed within a reasonable time.

does. The last thing you want is to be working with R & R people—mechanics who "Remove and Replace" parts without the slightest idea of what they are doing. Guess who picks up the bill for their ignorance?

Sometimes, despite the best efforts of individual and machine, the problem remains elusive. It may be a defect that occurs frequently in a particular model. If so, it may finally be figured out at the manufacturer by some very bright technician who specializes in problem-solving. The manufacturer will then issue a Technical Service Bulletin (TSB). If there is no TSB for your problem, the repair shop may have to call in the cavalry, in the form of the manufacturer's technical assistance department, to help.

Troubleshooting Computers

Due to the diversity and complexity of today's computerized systems, it is not practical to list probable causes of computer problems in a troubleshooting chart. Better to leave this task to the experts.

Frequently asked questions

Q How do I find out if a Technical Service Bulletin (TSB) has been issued for my car's computer problem?

A Ask the dealership nearest you or call the customer service representative's toll-free number listed in your owner's manual and in the Manufactures Directory in the appendix. If the TSB involves a safety-related problem, you can contact the National Highway Traffic Safety Administration's office in Washington, D.C. at (202) 366-2768. Many independent repair shops can also access this information by subscribing to a CD-ROM auto database. Finally, you can access the TBS Web site at: www.nhtsa.gov/cars/problems.

9
OIL

This chapter covers the most important (and what should be the most frequent) preventive maintenance chore for your car—checking and changing the oil. It also describes how to choose the right oil for your car and what those numbers (10W-30, etc.) on the oil container mean. Reading this chapter and following its advice will help you to avoid major engine failure.

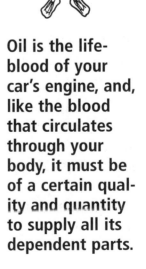

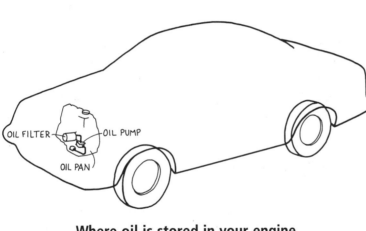

Where oil is stored in your engine

❖

Oil Cleans, Cools, and Lubricates

Oil is a jack-of-all-trades. It lubricates, it cleans, and it cools. It is the lifeblood of your car's engine, and, like the blood that circulates through your body, it must be of a certain quality and quantity to supply all of its dependent parts adequately. If the circulation is cut off because the fluid is too thick or too thin, or because a passageway is

Oil is the lifeblood of your car's engine, and, like the blood that circulates through your body, it must be of a certain quality and quantity to supply all its dependent parts.

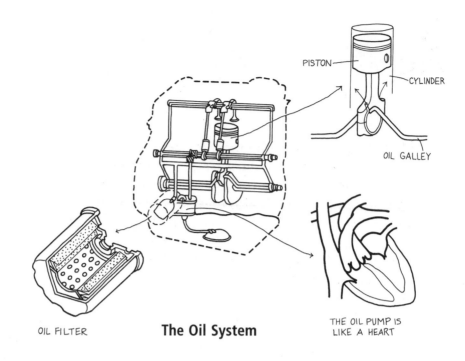

OIL FILTER   **The Oil System**   THE OIL PUMP IS LIKE A HEART

restricted, or because there is a leak somewhere in the system, it won't be long before damage (often irreparable) is done. Without oil, your engine's a goner. **Multigrade oils** have additives that keep oil flowing like cooking oil all year long.

How Oil Works

When the car is not in use, most of the oil sits in a metal **oil pan** attached to the bottom of the engine. As the ignition key is turned on, an **oil pump** pressurizes the oil and forces it through a screen. The screen catches large particles of dirt and grit. The oil is then pumped through the regular **oil filter**. The oil filter catches smaller bits of dirt and contaminants, the natural by-products of combustion, and stores them until the filter is changed.

From the filter, the oil is pushed through tiny enclosed passageways, or **oil galleys**, that are cut into the engine block. Now the oil moves to the bearings, connecting rods, and inside the cylinder walls, pistons, and

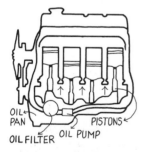

Oil is circulated around each of the cylinders, where it picks up some of the excess heat and carries it to the oil pan below.

valves, where it acts as a lubricant. It coats the metal parts with a thin film of fluid that acts as a slippery cushion.

Lubrication

In order for the metal moving parts of the engine to be efficient they have to fit tightly together. But without oil, the tightly fitting surfaces would quickly wear because metal against metal causes friction, friction causes heat, and heat causes wear.

At the same time that the oil is acting as a lubricant by separating the moving engine parts, it is providing another benefit as well: it is helping to cool the engine. Since it is a reasonably good conductor of heat, the oil picks up some of the excess heat as it flows around the hot combustion chambers and carries that heat to the oil pan below. This clever design works like clockwork if (1) the oil is at the proper level; (2) the oil is clean and of the correct weight (grade) and type; (3) the filter, pump, and other components are working properly; and (4) the passageways are not restricted.

Choosing the Right Oil

Because oil is as essential to an engine's health and well-being as blood is to our body's health, it must perform correctly. It has to flow easily enough to get up inside the cylinder walls and passageways. It must do this very quickly after the engine begins running, otherwise the metal parts will rub against each other without the lubrication they need.

To coat the internal parts adequately, oil should flow like cooking oil. Oil's consistency, however, changes in response to outside temperatures. Cold temperatures cause the oil to go from the consistency of cooking oil to that of honey. In this honey-like state, the oil might not reach the rapidly moving internal parts in time to separate and protect them. Warm temperatures cause the oil to thin out. It goes from the consistency of cooking oil to that of

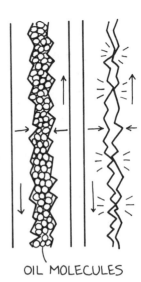

OIL MOLECULES

No matter how smooth a metal surface may appear, tiny irregularities exist that can cause friction. Oil separates and coats the metal moving parts so that they can slide smoothly over each other.

Note:

Most engine wear occurs within the first few moments after the car is started. Always let your car warm up a full minute.

In wintertime oil turns from the ideal consistency of cooking oil to that of honey. During summer, oil thins out to the consistency of vinegar.

❖

vinegar. In this state, the oil can't coat and separate the moving parts because it doesn't remain on them long enough. If it's too thick or too thin, the oil can't protect your engine.

For many years, the answer to temperature fluctuations was to change the weight of the oil in summer and

How to Read an Oil Can

The information printed on the oil container refers to the **viscosity** and weight (grade) of the oil. Letters such as **API** assure you that the oil meets the warranty standards set by the American Petroleum Institute (API) and the Society of Automotive Engineers (SAE). Numbers such as **10W-30** refer to viscosity, the oil's ability to flow at different temperatures. This ability is indicated by a range, 5 through 50. The smaller the number, the thinner the oil. **W** means that the oil is suitable for use in the winter. Letters such as **SJ** refer to the oil's quality. **S** means the oil is suitable for gasoline engines. **C** means it is suitable for diesel engines. High power engines are indicated by a higher letter—SH has better anti-wear additives than SG, for example. **Energy Conserving** means just that: this oil can help improve fuel economy.

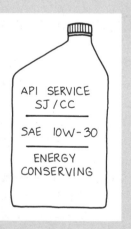

API SERVICE
SJ / CC

SAE 10W-30

ENERGY
CONSERVING

RECOMMENDED SAE   VISCOSITY GRADES

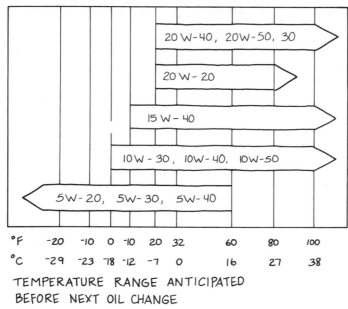

TEMPERATURE RANGE ANTICIPATED
BEFORE NEXT OIL CHANGE

Check your owner's manual for the correct oil weight for your car, and be sure to refer to the temperature range chart. It will tell you whether to change weights based on the season.

❖

in winter. As the temperature dropped, you would change from your car's normal weight oil for your car to a thinner one (from 40 to 30). The smaller the number, the thinner the oil. The thin oil was replaced with a thicker one as the temperature rose.

As petroleum product technology developed, **multi-grade oils** were developed. Additives were included in the oil to extend its working range. For example, additives gave an oil with a weight of 10W-30 the ability to flow freely at more than one temperature range—the 10W meant the oil was suitable for winter (that's what the "W" stands for) and the 30 meant it would also flow well in the summer. Check your owner's manual for the correct weight for your car, and be sure to refer also to the temperature range chart.

In the old days, people in cold climates often didn't drive their cars in the winter because of the great difficulty

Frequently asked questions

Q What does the word "lube" mean when I have my car's oil changed?

A "Lube" is a carryover from times when cars had many **fittings**, places where metal parts came together and had to be lubricated to prevent friction. Old grease is removed and new grease added. Some early models had as many as 63 fittings that had to be lubricated every time the motorist drove the vehicle! On today's vehicles, most of these fittings are sealed at the factory and no longer require any maintenance.

in starting them. Sometimes they even built a fire under the engine block to warm the engine oil so it would flow more easily. Another common practice was to drain the engine oil into a container and then bring it into the house and set it next to the wood stove, where it would be kept warm and remain thin enough to make starting easier. In the morning, it would be taken back out to the car and poured into the crankcase. What this method lacked in excitement it made up for in messiness.

Specialty Oils

Engine oils were traditionally made by refining or purifying petroleum. Scientists theorize that petroleum is the compressed remains of entire plant and animal civilizations long since buried and preserved in a state of decomposition.

For some years now, petroleum producers have been making engine oils from a synthetic base in a chemist's laboratory. These "designer" oils are able to reach moving parts more quickly than petroleum-based oils. They are especially suitable for extremely cold climates. Their ability to flow at very low temperatures is part of the rea-

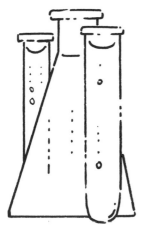

For some years now, petroleum producers have been making engine oils in the chemist's laboratory.

son, but they also resist breaking down or "shearing" under hard use. As oil cools and warms in response to changes in engine temperature, it loses both additives and consistency. Synthetics resist breakdown to a greater degree than traditional oils.

Making your car go the distance

With the rise in popularity of self-serve gas stations, we are required to perform more and more of our own routine maintenance. Smelling like *eau de gasoline* may never come into vogue, but if we ignore these maintenance procedures, the consequences may be premature wear of engine parts, resulting in expensive and unnecessary repair bills.

How and When to Check Oil

To check your oil, park on level ground and wait at least five minutes after turning off the engine. Or check the oil when the engine is cold.

1. Pull out the oil dipstick.
2. Wipe it down with a clean cloth.
3. Put the stick back in all the way, as close as possible to the angle at which it came out.
4. Pull it out again, and look at where the oil film lies on the stick in relation to the **add** and **full** lines.
5. If the film is below the **add** line, add a quart (liter) of the oil recommended in your owner's manual. If it is between the **add** and **full** lines, continue to check it regularly.
6. Repeat steps 1 through 5.

Changing the Oil and Filter

In order to get the maximum mileage out of your vehicle, have the oil changed every 3,500 miles (5,000 kilometers) or every spring, summer, winter, and fall. Always replace the filter when you have the oil changed.

Warning!
You may void a new car warranty if you use the wrong oil. Stick with your manufacturer's recommendation.

Even if your engine oil dipstick has been cleverly disguised by your manufacturer, it's important to find it so you can check the oil every time you add gas, or every other week.

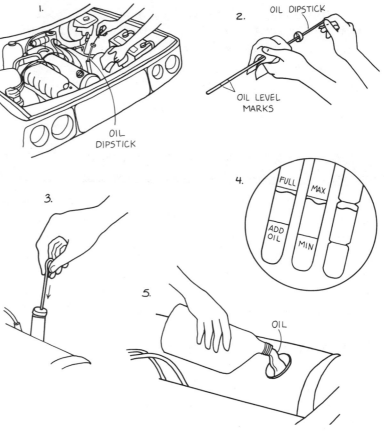

Warning!

An activated oil gauge or "idiot" light is a screaming, hopping call for help. The light is saying: "Oh driver, there's something happening down here, and I really think you should know about it!" Usually what's happening is that your engine parts are sautéing!

How to check your oil
❖

✓ Consult your owner's manual for the correct weight and quality of oil for your vehicle.

✓ Always ask for the specific oil recommended by your manufacturer. Do not assume the person doing the oil change will know.

✓ Keep track of how much oil your engine uses. It's the change in use that's important. If you notice a sudden change in oil consumption, you should have a professional look at your car.

✓ If you are driving a turbocharged or supercharged vehicle, use only a turbo-rated oil. They are specifi-

Money-Saving Tip

Make sure your oil level is high enough—but not too high. If there is too much oil, the engine seals, which means no oil escapes through the joints and they may burst, leaving you with an oil leak. Too much oil also raises the oil level to the point where the crankshaft actually rests in it. As the crankshaft turns, it whips the oil, adding air to it, just as an eggbeater would. The oil will have the consistency of egg whites: airy. Great for meringues, not good for engines. Airy oil loses its "stickability." It will reach the cylinder walls but it won't stay there. If the dipstick is reading significantly more than full, have it checked by a professional. Have the pan drained to the proper level, if necessary. Your engine will love you for it and live longer.

Too much oil is also bad for your engine. The oil turns into the consistency of beaten egg whites.

cally designed to handle the tremendous heat that is generated by a turbocharger or supercharger (see chapter 5 for more about superchargers). The carbon deposits that are formed while the engine cools down may coat the bearings and cause them to wear away at a fast and expensive rate. The extra protection of turbo-rated oils is necessary and well worth the additional cost.

Just as clogged arteries can cause serious health problems, unburned deposits from the engine eventually thicken the oil and coat the engine's inner parts, causing them to work harder and wear faster.

Troubleshooting the Oil System

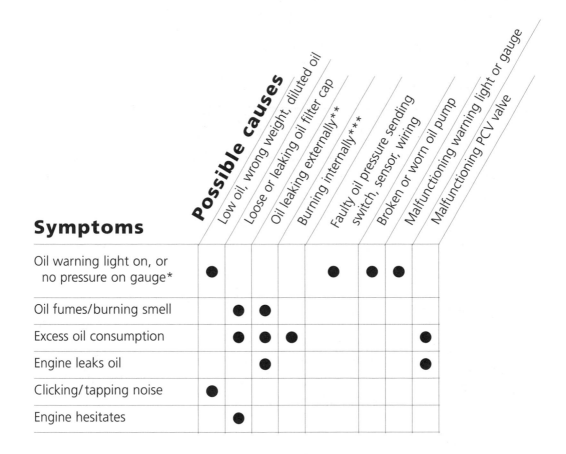

Symptoms	Low oil, wrong weight, diluted oil	Loose or leaking oil filter cap	Oil leaking externally**	Burning internally***	Faulty oil pressure sending switch, sensor, wiring	Broken or worn oil pump	Malfunctioning warning light or gauge	Malfunctioning PCV valve
Oil warning light on, or no pressure on gauge*	●				●	●	●	
Oil fumes/burning smell		●	●					
Excess oil consumption		●	●	●				●
Engine leaks oil			●					●
Clicking/tapping noise	●							
Engine hesitates		●						

*Danger! Don't drive the car!
**Could be leaking by loose oil filter, drain plug, gaskets, front or rear engine seal, worn valve components, rings or pistons or other engine parts
***Even the most difficult-to-find leaks can be detected with the use of a "black light" and special dye.

10
THE COOLING, HEATING, AND AIR-CONDITIONING SYSTEMS

Cooling system failures remain one of the major causes of highway breakdowns. In this chapter you'll learn how to keep your engine (and yourself) from overheating. You will also learn a few simple preventive maintenance steps that will help you to avoid the costly replacement of expensive cooling, heating, and air-conditioning components.

The cooling, heating, and air-conditioning systems

Just as the human body has sweat glands to help maintain the correct body temperature, the cooling system in a car's engine maintains the correct engine temperature range. It's your car's way of sweating.

Today's engines produce enough heat to warm a three-bedroom house.

The Engine Cooling System

Today's engines work harder and handle greater heat than ever before. The explosions taking place inside the engine produce temperatures in excess of 2,500° F (1,500° C)—enough heat to melt ordinary steel. That's also enough heat to warm a three-bedroom house on a freezing cold day. What you have under the hood of your car is a mini Dante's inferno.

Just as your body has an ideal temperature range, so does your car. Both are equipped with temperature control systems. When your body gets too hot, temperature sensors in your brain advise the body to sweat and the blood vessels to widen. More heat from the body passes through the skin into the air—that's how the body cools itself. If your body temperature rises significantly for a prolonged period of time, whether as a consequence of a fever or of sitting in the hot sun without a hat, damage may result—even death. Similarly, if the temperature of an engine rises beyond a certain point for a significant time, there is a high risk of damaging or destroying the engine.

Most cars are water-cooled. For these the cooling system depends on the flow of liquid called **coolant** (more about what coolant is later on) in and around the engine. There are, however, a few air-cooled engines, which depend on the flow of air in and around the engine, as well as on the cooling properties of oil. The most popular and efficient application of the air-cooled engine was in the Volkswagen Beetle.

How the Cooling System Works

The cooling system works in the following way:

A liquid called coolant is stored in the radiator, which consists of a metal tank and many narrow metal tubes which make up the **core**. A radiator cap seals the system and puts it under 14 to 18 pounds of pressure per square inch (PSI).

When the engine is running, a water pump that is powered by a belt attached to the engine draws coolant

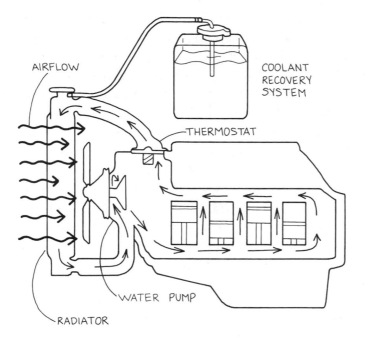

Cooling system components
❖

out of the radiator and into the engine compartment through a radiator hose. From there, it circulates through tiny copper-lined passageways that make up the engine's **water jacket**. As the coolant travels through the water jacket, it draws off heat.

The now-warm fluid flows back to the radiator via another hose, where it passes through a one-way, heat-sensitive door called a **thermostat**. Until the coolant reaches a predetermined temperature of about 180 to 205 degrees, the thermostat remains closed. This blocks the flow of coolant and forces it to recirculate around the combustion chambers. When the coolant finally reaches its normal operating temperature, the thermostat opens and the coolant flows back into the radiator. It then rushes down through the metal tubes where it is cooled—your car's equivalent of "sweating."

An electric fan or one powered by a belt which also serves the water pump pulls cool air from the outside through the radiator. The coolant is now ready to repeat its journey again and again.

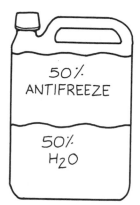

Coolant is a mixture of water and a chemical known as ethylene glycol, or antifreeze.

Most cars today have a coolant recovery system. As coolant heats up, it expands. The overflow is stored in a translucent plastic container, the overflow reservoir, attached to the radiator. When the engine is turned off, the coolant contracts and is drawn back into the radiator from the overflow reservoir.

Just as sweat consists of more than water and includes other body chemicals, coolant is also a combination of water and a weird-looking chemical known as ethylene glycol, or **antifreeze**. When mixed with water, antifreeze keeps the water in your radiator from boiling in summer and freezing in winter. The liquid in your car's radiator should always—365 days a year—be coolant.

The right proportion of water to antifreeze for your car can be found—you guessed it—in your owner's manual. This proportion determines the coolant's range of temperature protection. Often it's a 50:50 ratio, which will protect an engine from freezing down to -34° F (2° C) and raise its boiling point from 226° to 263° F (113° to 151° C). Only if you live in Deadhorse, Alaska (or an exceedingly cold climate) should the proportion of antifreeze to water be as high as 70:30. This will protect an engine down to -84° F (-64° C). More than 70 percent antifreeze causes the protective qualities of coolant to disappear.

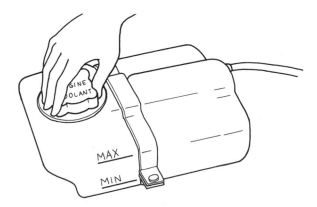

Without even removing the cap, you can see where the coolant is. If the coolant level is below the appropriate line, wait until the engine is cold, remove the cap on the reservoir, and add the mixture of antifreeze and water recommended in your owner's manual.

Making your car go the distance

The Cooling System

Assuming the correct level and proportion of coolant are maintained, and the water pump, thermostat, fan, and radiator cap are in working order, the correct temperature for the engine should be achieved. All it takes is a little TLC to make this driving dream a reality.

✓ Every other time you buy gas, or as often as each week during the summer, check to be sure there is plenty of coolant in the overflow reservoir.

✓ When topping off, use only antifreeze that states on the label "suitable for all engine types." This will ensure that it contains the special additives that protect all types of engine metals—aluminum as well as the more common cast iron.

✓ Be aware of changes in coolant consumption. If you are constantly replacing coolant, have the system inspected. Leaks don't always show up on your garage floor or in your driveway. Some leaks only occur when the engine is under the higher pressures of highway driving.

✓ Each year, get a professional maintenance check of the entire cooling system. The radiator, water pump, fan, thermostat, radiator cap, belts, hoses, clamps, and concentration of the antifreeze should be inspected. Any belt or hose that appears brittle, flaky, cracked, or mushy should be replaced at this time.

✓ Have the coolant system drained and flushed every two years. Most coolant loses its protective qualities eventually. When it does, water pumps and radiators deteriorate. The exception applies to cars built after 1996 with "extended-wear coolant." Check with your dealer or owner's manual to learn whether your car has extended-wear coolant.

Warning!

Never open the coolant reservoir or remove the radiator cap until you are absolutely certain the engine is cold. If the cap is removed while the engine is hot, the coolant could burst out of the radiator and the escaping steam could injure you.

Slow-moving traffic in summer can cause even the healthiest cooling system to overheat.

✓ The amount of coolant that is right for your car can be found in your owner's manual under "Liquid Capacity" or "Specifications."

When Something Goes Wrong with the Cooling System

If your engine does overheat (your engine "temp" light goes on, or the temperature gauge moves into the "hot" zone), there are several things you can do to keep the repair bill somewhere below the national deficit.

1) Turn off the air-conditioning; it makes the engine work 20 percent hotter; **2)** turn your car's heater to its hottest setting; **3)** turn the heater fan on. This will pull some of the heat away from the engine and into the passenger compartment. This might also be a good time to open the windows. Of course, now *you* will overheat, but remember, dry cleaning your suit is cheaper than rebuilding your engine. **4)** try to increase the distance between you and the car directly in front of you. Its tailpipe is sending out hot exhaust fumes that are making a bad problem worse.

If it's hot enough to stir-fry on the pavement, none of these strategies may help. If all else fails and your car is still overheating, it's time to turn your hazard lights on, get the car safely off the road, and turn the engine off and let it cool down.

If, after letting the system cool down, you check and find nothing apparently wrong, it is usually safe to drive the car, assuming the engine temperature or coolant indicator is normal. You may not even need to consult a technician.

Like a jogger who runs too many miles on a hot day and experiences heat exhaustion, your car may sometimes need to rest in the shade and get its fluid balance back. Listen to your car as you would to your body. Respond by giving each system a rest and replacing lost fluids before returning to a normal routine. Should the car continue to overheat, you probably have a more serious problem.

The Heating System

On some especially chilly winter days, it may feel like it takes forever to get yourself and your windshield defrosted. But, in fact, our modern automotive heating systems are models of efficiency and comfort, particularly in comparison with earlier heating methods. In the early days of motoring one had to be quite ingenious to overcome the sting of the elements. Pans of glowing briquettes were often placed on the floor in the passenger compartment; all kinds of wild motoring outfits were designed. Even as late as 1930, being comfortable inside a car in cold weather was considered a luxury.

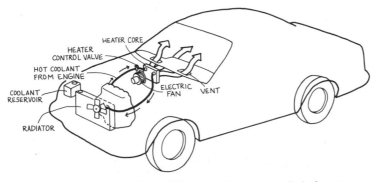

The heating system. The different heater and defroster controls allow you to open and close the passageways leading inside the car, directing the heat to different places in the passenger compartment—up to the windshield for defrost, down to the passengers for comfort.

❖

If your car really is taking forever to warm up on a cold morning, blame the cooling system, not the heater, for it is the coolant that actually warms you. The heater is actually a mini radiator and works in a similar way. When you turn on the heater/defroster button or lever in your car, heated coolant is diverted from its normal journey. Instead of flowing from the engine to the radiator, where most of its heat would have been released, the coolant is drawn by the water pump through a **heater control valve** (a one-way door) to a smaller radiator called the **heater core**, located directly in front of the

A. C. Principles

(A) WHEN A LIQUID BECOMES A VAPOR (GAS), IT ABSORBS HEAT.

(B) WHEN A VAPOR BECOMES A LIQUID IT GIVES OFF HEAT.

(C) HEAT ALWAYS MOVES FROM A WARMER SPOT TO A COLDER SPOT

passenger compartment. The hot coolant passes through the core and releases its heat. An electric fan then forces the warmth of the coolant into the passenger compartment through passageways called *ducts*.

The Air-conditioning System

Air-conditioning doesn't add cold; it removes heat. It accomplishes this by removing heat from one area and sending it to another through the use of a fluid called **refrigerant**. This process of absorbing and releasing heat is what cools the inside of our cars, our homes, and our refrigerators.

Although individual components may vary from car to car, the following basics apply to all air-conditioning systems.

Refrigerant has a unique characteristic: it needs very little heat to bring it to a boil. In a car, refrigerant is circulated through an **evaporator**, or series of coils, located in front of the passenger compartment. An **expansion valve** (a one-way door) regulates the flow of refrigerant into the evaporator. As the refrigerant moves through the evaporator, it boils and absorbs heat from inside the car.

From the evaporator, the heated refrigerant moves to

Air-conditioning doesn't add cold; it removes heat.

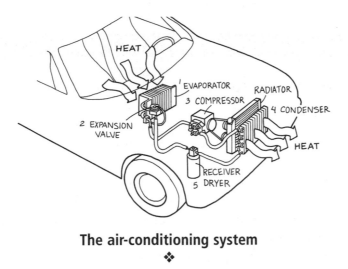

The air-conditioning system
❖

the **compressor**, a belt-driven pump. The compressor compresses the gas under extremely high pressure, dramatically raising the temperature of the refrigerant to more than 150° F (118° C).

From the compressor, the refrigerant goes to the **condenser**, which looks like a radiator and sits in front of the regular radiator. In the condenser, air cools the refrigerant and returns it to a liquid state. Just as it absorbed heat when it boiled, it now gives up its heat as it turns back

Money-Saving Tip

To keep your air-conditioning in good working order, run it for about five minutes once a week whenever the outside temperature is above 50° F (10° C). The many rubber components of this system dry out and crack if they are not lubricated by the oil that circulates with the refrigerant. This lubrication only takes place when the air-conditioning is turned on.

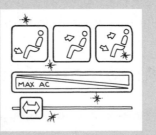

Frequently asked questions

Q Does it matter if an engine runs cold?

A You bet it does—and the consequences can be serious. Engines that do not reach their "ideal" temperatures retain moisture and do not burn off the by-products of combustion—carbon deposits. These deposits build up inside engines causing excess stress, heat, and premature engine wear. There are a number of reasons why an engine will run cold. Two of the most common causes are a faulty thermostat that never closes (and so the coolant never warms adequately) and a low coolant level. Poor fuel economy usually accompanies a cold engine.

into a liquid. As a high pressure liquid once again, the refrigerant flows to the **receiver dryer**, a filter that removes any moisture from the liquid. Air-conditioning units hate moisture. A blower motor forces this cooled air into the car through vents.

Known for many years as Freon, a chemical in the chlorofluorocarbons group, the refrigerant R-12 was the medium of choice for air-conditioning systems. But research has now shown that it contributes to the depletion of the earth's ozone layer. In its place the refrigerant R134a, a CFC-free refrigerant, has been substituted. From now on the refrigerant installed in all new vehicles will be R134a. *Note:* The two cannot be mixed. Using the wrong kind can damage the air-conditioning unit.

Many of today's cars are equipped with a computer that controls temperatures in the passenger compartment.

Automatic Climate Control

The first attempts at air-conditioning required bulky systems to provide the passenger compartment with cool air on a hot day. Today's systems are more streamlined.

Many cars are now equipped with a computer that controls passenger compartment temperatures. Electronic sensors detect temperatures within the passenger compartment and feed that information to the computer. The computer compares these temperatures against preset "ideal" temperatures. If the sensors register colder, the computer then directs an appropriate amount of warmed coolant to the passenger compartment. It also automatically opens and closes heating vents to allow just the right amount of warm air into the passenger compartment. When it's warm outside, the temperature control system also operates the air-conditioning. Today, heating, air-conditioning, and engine cooling are all tied together.

Making your car go the distance
Temperature Control Systems

✔ To cool properly, the air-conditioning system must have the correct amount of refrigerant. This amount is specific to your car and needs to be recharged periodically. Most modern shops recharge by capturing the old refrigerant and recycling it.

✔ Have all air-conditioning components inspected according to the service schedule in your owner's manual.

✔ Conversions to R134a are currently being developed by the manufacturers and differ widely from car to car. Check with your dealership to determine if there is any warranty coverage.

Warning!

Fixing the air-conditioning system is a job for a properly equipped professional. The refrigerant boils at a very low temperature and can easily burn the skin. In contact with a flame or other heat source, it can change into a poisonous gas. And adding too much freon can result in an explosion.

Troubleshooting the Cooling System

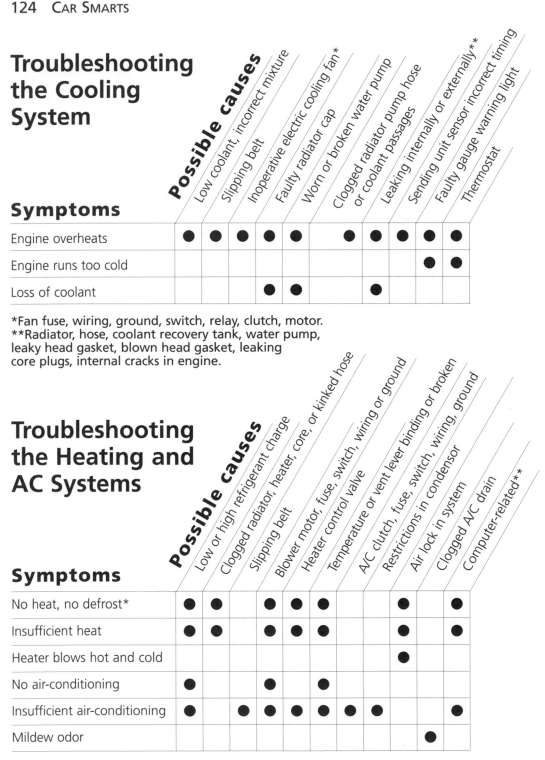

Symptoms	Low coolant, incorrect mixture	Slipping belt	Inoperative electric cooling fan*	Faulty radiator cap	Worn or broken water pump	Clogged radiator pump hose or coolant passages	Leaking internally or externally**	Sending unit sensor incorrect timing	Faulty gauge warning light	Thermostat
Engine overheats	●	●	●	●	●	●	●	●	●	●
Engine runs too cold									●	●
Loss of coolant				●	●		●			

*Fan fuse, wiring, ground, switch, relay, clutch, motor.
**Radiator, hose, coolant recovery tank, water pump, leaky head gasket, blown head gasket, leaking core plugs, internal cracks in engine.

Troubleshooting the Heating and AC Systems

Symptoms	Low or high refrigerant charge	Clogged radiator, heater, core, or kinked hose	Slipping belt	Blower motor, fuse, switch, wiring or ground	Heater control valve	Temperature or vent lever binding or broken	A/C clutch, fuse, switch, wiring or ground	Restrictions in condensor	Air lock in system	Clogged A/C drain	Computer-related**
No heat, no defrost*	●	●		●	●	●			●		●
Insufficient heat	●	●		●	●	●			●		●
Heater blows hot and cold									●		
No air-conditioning	●			●			●				
Insufficient air-conditioning	●		●	●	●	●	●	●			●
Mildew odor										●	

*If you are experiencing defroster difficulty in your imported vehicle:
1. Move the air intake lever or button to "fresh"
2. Turn the blower on high setting
3. Set the temp control to "hot"
4. Switch the air conditioner to "on." See if the defroster works now

**On vehicles with electronic climate control, a technician will need to follow the manufacturer's service manual for diagnosing problems.

11
THE DRIVE TRAIN

Whether you drive a rear-wheel, front-wheel, four-wheel, or all-wheel drive vehicle, the transmissions that transmit power from the engine to the wheels are complex, and their repairs can be expensive. Learning about them will help you to avoid a shiftless transmission. With the right preventive maintenance you can expect smaller and fewer repair bills.

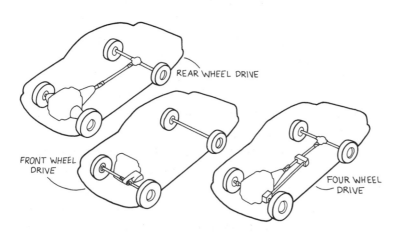

In a rear-wheel drive car, only the rear wheels receive power. In a front-wheel drive car, only the front wheels receive power. In four-wheel and all-wheel drive cars, however, all four wheels receive power.

❖

The drive train consists of those components that pass along or transmit power from the engine to the wheels. In most cars only two wheels receive power. While drive trains vary in their design, there are a number of components that are common to all. These include *transmissions*

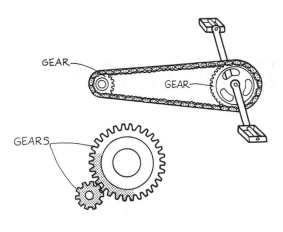

Gears are round metal wheels with teeth.

❖

and the metal linkage that connects the transmission to the wheels.

Let's return to the analogy of the bicyclist for a moment. Remember that it was through the bicycle chain that the energy produced by the pumping action of the bicyclist's legs was passed along to the bicycle wheels? Look more closely at that bicycle chain and you will see a series of round metal toothed wheels that we call gears. Peel back the skin of most transmissions and you will also find a series of gears.

Gears are necessary because cars and bicyclists are subject to **inertia**, the force that places resistance on a car's forward motion from a dead stop. However, once the car is moving, its heavy weight, which had made it so difficult to move initially, is now the factor that keeps it moving. **Momentum** has taken over.

To compensate for these natural forces, cars need slow, powerful turns from their wheels to get started and when traveling up hills. But they need speedy turns from their wheels when they're traveling at normal highway speeds. To meet the changing needs of the car, the energy produced by the engine has to be transmitted differently to the car's wheels—sometimes powerfully, sometimes speedily, sometimes not at all. The gears inside the transmission make it possible to meet those different needs. The transmission is the "link" between the engine and the wheels.

"GEARS WORK on the PRINCIPLE THAT THE FASTER THE ENGINE TURNS IN RELATION TO THE Wheels THE MORE POWER (TORQUE) IS PRODUCED"

How Gears Work

Gears are always found in sets. Assuming that their teeth are meshed together, when one gear turns the other gear also turns. To see how gears really work, let's start with first gear. Let's assume the big gear with 40 teeth is attached to the wheels, and the small gear with ten teeth is attached to the engine. How many times will the small gear go around in the time it takes the large gear to go around once? If you answered "four," you rocket to the head of the class. The effort of four speedy turns of the engine is transferred into one powerful turn of the wheel. This relationship is expressed as a **gear ratio**. The gear ratio for this set of gears is 4:1. This gear ratio works well for a car that is starting out from a dead stop because it provides the greatest amount of torque or twisting power from the engine to the wheels. The "lower" the gear, the more power and less speed is delivered to the wheels.

As the car continues to move forward, having broken with the force of inertia, it needs less power and more speed. In second gear, the gear attached to the wheels may have 30 teeth and the gear attached to the engine may have ten teeth. Three speedy turns of the input shaft are transferred into one slower turn of the output shaft

1st GEAR

2nd GEAR

3rd GEAR

4th GEAR

5th GEAR

Gears are always found in sets. Here are gears one through five.

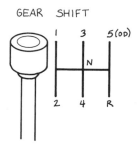

GEAR SHIFT

With a manual transmission, you select the gear appropriate for the driving conditions.

(gear ratio 3:1). Second gear is still a powerful gear but not as powerful as first. Eventually, when the car reaches highway speeds, the force of momentum has taken over. Consequently, in fourth (depending on the gear box), both gears are turning at the same speed (gear ratio 3:3). All cars have at least three gears, plus reverse, and many have four, five, or even six.

Manual Transmissions

There are two types of transmissions: manual (standard) and automatic. With a manual or standard transmission, you select the gear appropriate for the driving conditions by moving a gear shift or lever. With an automatic transmission the gears are selected for you.

The earliest gears actually moved into and out of each other, sometimes meshing smoothly, sometimes not. When two gears meshed together their separate movements had to be coordinated or—*crunch, crunch*—the gear teeth bumped into each other. The result was missing teeth and frequent gear replacement. Then came synchronizers.

Synchronizers are rings with teeth that point out ("dogs") and collars with teeth that point in. It is the synchronizers that actually move, not the gears. The gear

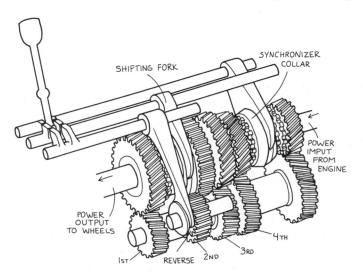

A manual transmission

Frequently asked questions

Q What is fifth gear, or an **overdrive** gear?

A In a **manual** (standard) **transmission**, a fifth gear (or an overdrive gear in an automatic transmission) takes advantage of the car's momentum. When being driven at highway speeds, a car needs speed, not power. It requires fewer crankshaft turns from the engine. Since the engine doesn't work as hard, it doesn't use as much gas. Consequently, you save money by using fifth gear, or overdrive, at highway speeds.

ratios are already locked together. This makes for smooth shifting, few crunches, and very little wear on the gears themselves. Thus, the gears rarely wear out; the synchronizers do instead. Such a deal.

The Clutch

If your car has a manual transmission, it also has a **clutch**. Located between the engine and the transmission, the clutch makes it possible for the engine to change gears. The clutch connects and disconnects the engine from the rest of the drive train. By disconnecting the transmission from the engine, the clutch allows the engine to continue to run without transmitting its power to the wheels.

How the Clutch Works

Clutch designs vary, but most have the same basic components—the flywheel, several steel plates or discs that slide along a shaft, a round metal doughnut called a

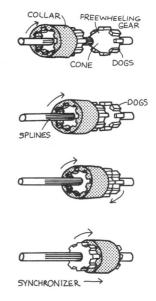

Synchronizers are rings with teeth that point out and collars with teeth that point in. It is the synchronizers that actually move, not the gears.

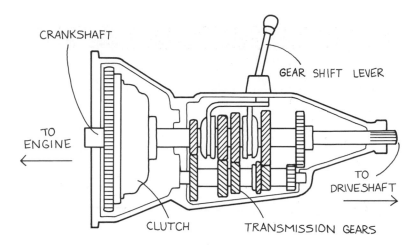

The clutch connects and disconnects the engine from the wheels.

❖

throw-out bearing, and a metal arm called a **release fork**. As you know from chapter 5, the flywheel is attached to the crankshaft (the bar that holds onto the pistons). Next in line is a plate called the **clutch disc**, which is covered with a tough layer of friction material, and finally there is the **pressure plate**. A throw-out bearing and a release fork secure the components to the shaft.

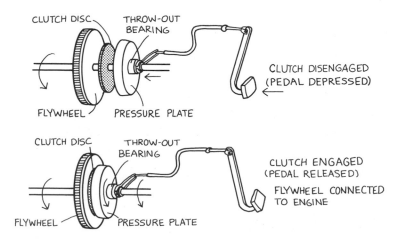

When the clutch pedal is released, the engine and wheels are connected. When the clutch pedal is depressed, the engine is disconnected from the wheels.

When the clutch pedal is released, the pressure plate squeezes the clutch disc against the flywheel. Consequently, the clutch begins to turn at the same rate as the flywheel. The engine is now connected to the transmission and the wheels.

When the clutch pedal is depressed, the engine is disconnected from the wheels. Consequently, the clutch disc, which had been squeezed against the flywheel, separates from it. The transmission is now in neutral. Power will not flow to the wheels until the clutch pedal is released again.

The clutch disc

Automatic Transmissions

In an automatic transmission, the gears are shifted automatically. Instead of a clutch, an automatic transmission has a **torque converter**.

The torque converter is a housing filled with two fans and a lightweight oil called **transmission fluid**. One fan is

Money-Saving Tip

Depending on the gear selected, the clutch disc will go from rest (zero turns) or no revolutions per minute (rpms) to as many as 5,000 rpms or more in a fraction of a second! Just before the connection with the flywheel is complete, the disc experiences a slipping motion that results in friction. Friction causes heat and heat causes wear.

Do not use your clutch pedal for a foot rest. It makes a very bad one. "Riding the clutch" causes the clutch disc to slip, which causes friction and can burn out a clutch in a short period of time. Keep your foot off the clutch pedal when not in use; engage it and disengage it quickly.

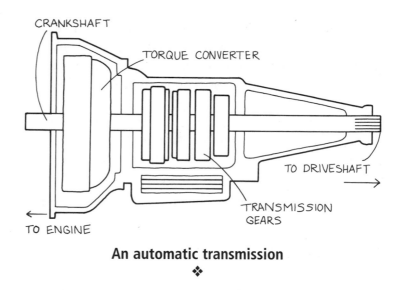

An automatic transmission

❖

called an **impeller** and is attached to the engine. The other fan is called a **turbine** and is attached to the transmission. As the engine's crankshaft rotates, the impeller turns. If the impeller is turning fast enough, the other fan turns. The more speed the engine develops, the faster the fans spin.

The fans' motion pressurizes the fluid within tiny passageways in the **valve control body**. Here the fluid moves a series of metal components called bands (collars) and clutches which change the gears. All the driver has to do is to step on the gas.

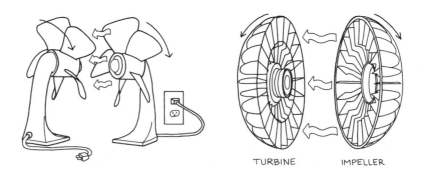

How the torque converter works: when the plugged-in fan is turned on, it blows air into the second fan, causing it to turn. This is analogous to the action of the impeller on the turbine.

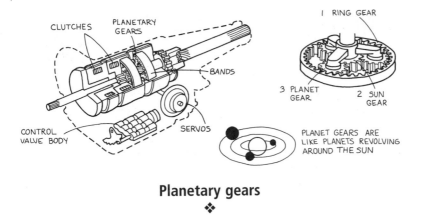

Planetary gears

❖

Planetary Gears

The gears within an automatic transmission are called **planetary gears**. They may not look like the ones within a manual transmission, but the principle is the same: sets of gears (two, three, four, or more, depending on the gearbox, plus reverse) provide the necessary speed or power appropriate for different driving conditions.

In an automatic transmission, the gears move around each other in a circle. Each gear set consists of an outer **ring gear** within which sits a central **sun gear** flanked by smaller planet gears. Just as you might expect, these smaller planet gears move around the sun gear. Gears are selected by locking and releasing specific gear sets.

Electronically Controlled Transmissions

Many of today's transmissions are computer controlled and remarkably efficient. These "smart" transmissions use a computer to track input from several different sources, including the pressure on the accelerator pedal, and crunch the data as many as 30 times per second. The computer can recognize a quick accelerator movement and downshift at just the right time—as efficiently as

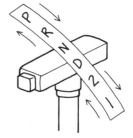

With an automatic transmission, the gears are selected for you.

Money-Saving Tip

Never rock your car back and forth in a snow bank more than a few times. It overheats the transmission.

most drivers could do manually. Some very smart electronic transmissions can memorize a driver's habits. In addition, many of the cost benefits that were traditionally associated with the fuel economy of manual transmissions are quickly disappearing as electronic transmissions use the speed of computers to do our shifting for us.

Final Drive for the Rear-Wheel Drive Car

Final drive includes the components that finish or finalize the transmission of power from the engine to the wheels. **Rear-wheel drive** vehicles transmit power only to the rear wheels. Front-wheel drive vehicles transmit power only to the front wheels. Four-wheel and all-wheel drive vehicles can transmit power to all four wheels, providing awesome grip.

In a rear-wheel drive vehicle, power is transferred from the transmission to the car's rear wheels via a long turning bar or shaft, called a **driveshaft**. The driveshaft is attached to the **differential**. This special set of gears does two things: (1) It takes the power of the engine and transmission and turns it at a right angle to the rear axles that connect the rear wheels. (2) The differential allows the wheels to travel at different speeds when cornering. This is necessary because the outer wheels follow a larger arc than the inner wheels when the vehicle turns. Spreading the engine transmission and differential out along the entire length of the vehicle results in more space for the rugged components associated with towing or hauling heavy loads.

Final Drive for the Front-Wheel Drive Car

In a **front-wheel drive** car, the differential is moved forward and combined with the transmission into one unit called the **transaxle**. Power follows a more indirect path before it reaches the shorter axles (stub axles) that are connected to the front wheels. Placing the heavy engine and transmission over the front "driving" wheels results in additional grip on wet and slippery surfaces and extra passenger space.

Four-Wheel Drive

In recent years the technology that transfers power to all four wheels has led to a whole generation of **four-wheel drive** passenger cars and light trucks from which to choose. Not only are there many manufacturers designing four-wheel drive vehicles, but they are doing it in several different ways.

Traditional part-time four-wheel drive transfers

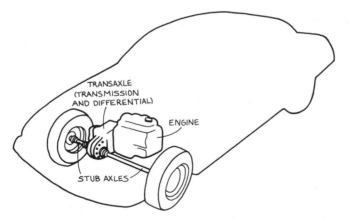

In a front-wheel-drive car, the differential is moved forward and combined with the transmission into one unit called the transaxle.

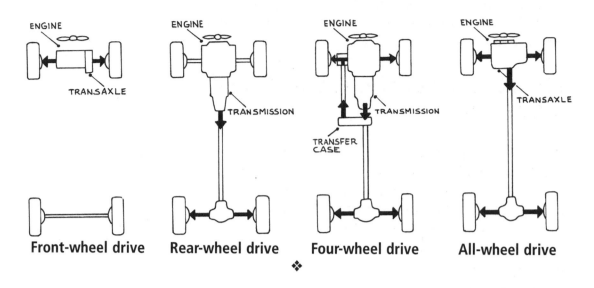

Front-wheel drive   Rear-wheel drive   Four-wheel drive   All-wheel drive

power to the rear wheels through a differential. It can also transfer power to all four wheels through a **transfer case**. This special third set of gears, which is typically engaged through a shift lever, can lock the front and rear axles together. When power is transferred to all four wheels, traction is increased. The system is designed for use on road surfaces with some "give" (gravel, snow, ice). Extended dry pavement use can result in damage to the components.

Modern four-wheel-drive vehicles have an interior shift lever to make locking and unlocking the two axles easy and convenient. To make them even more convenient, a number of systems have been developed which allow the driver to shift into four-wheel drive while the vehicle is moving.

All-Wheel Drive

There are several types of all-wheel-drive systems. These systems use electronics to transfer power where it is most needed.

With **all-wheel drive**, sometimes called **full-time four-wheel drive**, power goes to all four wheels all the time, giving extra traction on slippery surfaces as well as dry roads. The power split is usually 40 percent to the front axle and 60 percent to the rear, but it can be 90 percent to the front and 10 percent to the rear.

In some all-wheel-drive systems, power goes to two wheels until wheel spin is sensed, at which point power is directed to the opposite set of wheels or whichever wheels need it. The result is exceptional grip on any type of road surface without the added fuel consumption of most four-wheel-drive systems.

U-joints and CV Joints

Universal joints, or "U-joints," are metal joints designed like human wrists. In a rear-wheel or four-wheel drive vehicle, these coupling mechanisms facilitate movement between the transmission and the driveshaft and the differential. To see how U-joints work, keep your arm still and wave your hand up and down. The wrist motion is a simple flex, isn't it? Your hand is ideally designed with ligaments and muscles to help you perform this flexing motion many, many times without you having to do anything to maintain it. But a U-joint, because it's metal, needs a special lubricant for

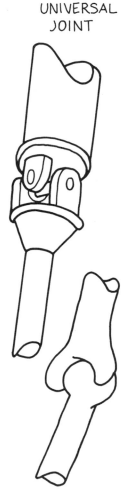

UNIVERSAL JOINT

HUMAN JOINT

U-joints are metal joints designed like human joints.

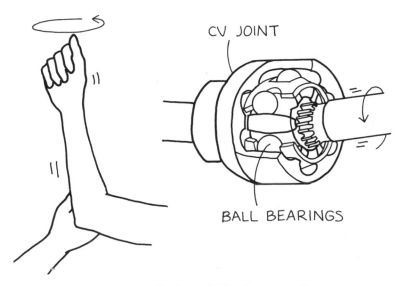

CV JOINT

BALL BEARINGS

CV joints are designed like human elbows.

Money-Saving Tip

A CV joint often warns us of problems by a clicking sound that comes from the front wheels, typically when the car is turning a corner. If you hear this warning sound, have the CV joints inspected by a professional for damage as soon as possible. If a slight tear in the boot is discovered early enough, you may only have to replace it, not the joint. Replacing the boot is much less expensive than replacing a failed joint.

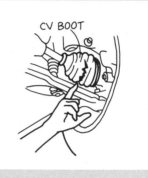

protection. A thick dark grease coats the joint to prevent friction from causing premature wear. U-joints are now pre-lubed and sealed at the factory (as are most other couplers).

The front-wheel drive version of a U-joint is a **CV** (constant velocity) **joint**. CV joints are designed like human elbows. On front-wheel drive cars, the short or "stub" axles must be able to transfer the up-and-down motion of the road as well as the side-to-side motion of the steering. Consequently, a more complicated connector is required. CV joints are the answer. To see how a CV joint works, hold your right elbow in your left palm and rotate it. Now compare that motion to the simple flexing motion of your wrist. The more complex the motion, the more complex the mechanism. The expensive-to-replace ball bearings inside the CV joints are protected with lubricating grease and sealed with rubber covers called boots.

The Drive Train

If transmissions sound complex, they are. If they sound like they could be expensive to fix, they can be. *But* they don't have to be. Here are a few ways to avoid transmission problems.

✓ Limit the weight you carry on long trips even if it means shipping some things—particularly if you are driving into the mountains. Carrying a heavy load, especially uphill, can cause a transmission to overheat, and overheating is a major cause of transmission damage.

✓ Much transmission damage occurs in the morning before the transmission fluid has reached the hundreds of delicate metal parts. Jumping in your car and throwing it in reverse is one sure way to harm a transmission. Give the car a full minute to warm up before you put it in gear.

Overloading and overtowing can cause transmission damage.

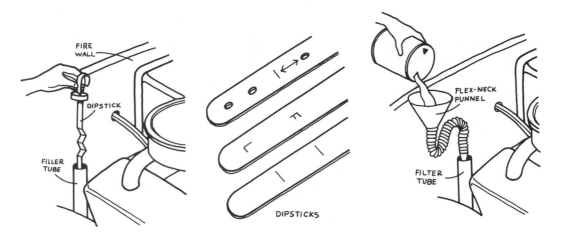

The proper procedure for checking automatic transmission fluid varies from car to car. Your owner's manual tells you how. In the method shown above:

1. Locate the transmission dipstick (usually a different color than the oil dipstick)

2. Pull it from the tube and wipe it with a clean rag

3. Reinsert the dipstick

4. Pull it out again and read the fluid level

5. If the fluid is low, you will need a special funnel (available in auto parts stores). Use only the fluid recommended by the manufacturer.

6. Pour fluid through the funnel. Caution: do not overfill.

❖

 Check the automatic transmission fluid level or have it checked once a month. In addition to making your transmission shift correctly, transmission fluid protects the delicate internal parts from wear.

 When you know the car will have a difficult task, like lugging a heavy load uphill, choose a lower gear. Read your owner's manual for an explanation of how to use these gears. Your transmission will appreciate it.

 If you are doing a lot of severe driving (towing a trailer, for example), consider having your car equipped with a extra transmission cooler. (Check your owner's manual for any special requirements.)

✓ Don't shift into park or reverse until the vehicle has come to a complete stop.

✓ Have the transmission and clutch (if appropriate) adjusted to manufacturer's specifications. Doing so reduces wear, improves performance, and helps you to avoid expensive repairs.

✓ Have your CV boots checked for damage whenever the car is up on a lift. It's a simple visual check that only takes a minute but can save you hundreds of dollars.

✓ Have the transmission fluid, final-drive fluids, and the transmission filter changed as often as your owner's manual recommends.

✓ Manual transmission fluid, final-drive fluid, and transfer case fluids should be checked by a professional every six months or as often as your owner's manual recommends. All are easily checked while the car is on a lift.

Don't tear out of the driveway as soon as you start your engine. Give your car a full minute to warm up before you put it in gear.

Troubleshooting the Drive Train

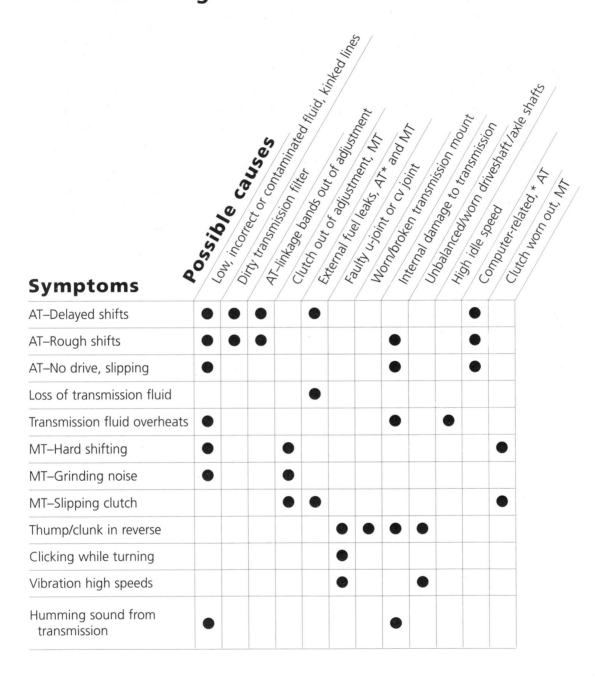

Symptoms	Low, incorrect or contaminated fluid, kinked lines	Dirty transmission filter	AT–linkage bands out of adjustment	Clutch out of adjustment, MT	External fluid leaks, AT* and MT	Faulty u-joint or cv joint	Worn/broken transmission mount	Internal damage to transmission	Unbalanced/worn driveshaft/axle shafts	High idle speed	Computer-related,* AT	Clutch worn out, MT
AT–Delayed shifts	●	●	●		●						●	
AT–Rough shifts	●	●	●					●			●	
AT–No drive, slipping	●							●			●	
Loss of transmission fluid					●							
Transmission fluid overheats	●							●		●		
MT–Hard shifting	●			●								●
MT–Grinding noise	●			●								
MT–Slipping clutch				●	●							●
Thump/clunk in reverse						●	●	●	●			
Clicking while turning						●						
Vibration high speeds						●			●			
Humming sound from transmission	●							●				

Possible causes

AT–Automatic
MT–Manual or standard
*Seals, gaskets, lines

12 STEERING AND SUSPENSION

This chapter describes how suspension and steering work together to help your vehicle hold the road. The more responsive your vehicle is, the safer it is. Repair done to suspension and steering systems, often referred to as "front end" work, is one area in which consumers are at higher than normal risk of being overcharged and sold unnecessary work. In this chapter, you will learn how to avoid that fate.

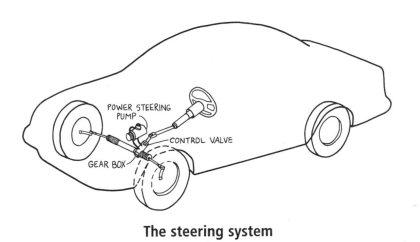

The steering system

❖

Steering and suspension are kindred spirits. **Steering** is about controlling the right, left, and straight directional movements of your car; **suspension** is about controlling its up-and-down movement as it travels over the uneven road surface. These two systems not only share some of the same components, they each contribute to the other's

The steering and suspension systems are analogous to the wrists, elbows, and knees of the human body.

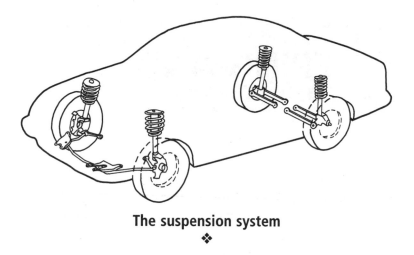

The suspension system

❖

performance. They also affect your safety since they heavily influence a car's "handling."

Rack and Pinion Steering

"Rack and pinion" may sound like a method of medieval torture, but it's really the popular, compact, and lightweight steering mechanism found in most modern cars. Rack and pinion steering eliminates the traditional steer-

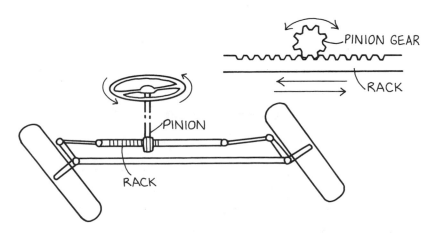

Rack and pinion steering eliminates the traditional steering gearbox and replaces it with a simpler set of gears.

ing gearbox and replaces it with a simpler set of gears: a toothed wheel called a **pinion gear** is attached to the end of the steering shaft, where it meets a long bar, or rack, that also has teeth. Rods and levers called **tie rods** and **steering arms** attach the rack to the wheels.

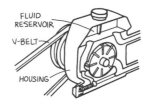

Power Steering

In the early days, cars ran on very narrow tires and were extremely responsive to the least guidance from the steering wheel. Driving these cars may have been easy on the driver's arms but not so on their legs, for the driver and passengers often walked home after the car skittered off the road. To be up close and personal with ditches was not a desired condition, but it was a frequent one.

Power steering uses a pump driven by a belt to pressurize fluid. If the belts break, you can still steer, but you will need to use more muscle.

Money-Saving Tip

Rack and pinion systems are bathed in lubricant and protected by coverings called **boots**. Rubber seals keep the lubricant in and the dirt out. Like most rubber, the seals shrink and crack with age, especially in cold weather. If you notice the steering wheel is hard to turn on cold mornings, have the steering inspected. A bit of special lubricant applied by a professional and specifically made for revitalizing seals may help. If the steering rack is faulty, you may even be entitled to special goodwill compensation from your manufacturer if this is a well-known problem.

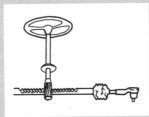

Boots and seals in the rack and pinion system can shrink and crack with age.

Steering and suspension influence a car's handling.

With the introduction and acceptance of wider tires, vehicles stayed on the road better, but they were more difficult to park in small spaces. Parking a car weighing more than 2,000 pounds became a chore fit only for weightlifters.

Power steering adds the turning power of the engine to the turning power of the steering gears. This assistance comes from a belt-driven **power steering pump**. This pump pressurizes the power steering fluid, which is held in a reservoir. The fluid pressure increases turning power. Consequently, less manual pressure is needed to turn the steering wheel.

If the belt for the pump breaks or the fluid in the reservoir is too low, the power assist may be lost. You will still be able to steer, but you'll have to really crank on that steering wheel to get it to turn.

Variable Ratio Power Steering (Computer Assisted)

One side effect of power assist is a diminished sense of connection to the road. To compensate, some manufacturers now electronically reduce the power assist to the steering when you're traveling at highway speeds, where the extra boost is not needed, and reinstate it when you're traveling at slower speeds. This **variable ratio power** steering makes it easy to park without losing that good "road feel" when driving.

Suspension

The suspension system supports the body and chassis and attaches them to the wheels. Suspension is also the system that gives us a nice comfortable ride. Were it not for your car's suspension, every time you went over a bump, the car would bounce, and bounce, and bounce. Ad nauseam. But the suspension is even more important to your safety than to your comfort. The suspension components help to keep the tires in constant contact with the road.

For many years automobiles were designed "body-

Suspension helps to control vehicle ride.

❖

on-frame"—a metal body that included the passenger compartment, hood, trunk, and fenders was attached to a steel frame that included the power train, steering, and suspension. Most vehicles today use a frameless "uni-body" design; both frame and body are made of metal panels that are welded together. These changes have made cars far more comfortable and airtight. They have also made simple suspension components not so simple.

Comfort and Control

The suspension's job is to provide passengers with the most comfortable ride and drivers with the best possible road handling. Suspension designs vary widely, but they include similar components: **springs**, **shock absorbers**, **struts**, and metal arms. These parts, often assisted by a computer, are combined in various sizes and shapes in both the front and the rear of the car.

The difference between the front and rear suspension components is largely determined by their task. Since the rear wheels don't steer, they have fewer angles to contend with. But the amount of weight that has to be distributed properly by the rear suspension varies more than it does for the front. And in rear-wheel drive cars, the rear also has to transfer the turning power of the engine.

Before the days of rubber tires, every bump from every rock and uneven bit of roadway was transferred

Most vehicles today use a frameless "uni-body" design, which means that both frame and body are made of panels that are welded together.

directly through the wheels to the seats. With the development of air-filled rubber tires, passengers were isolated from rough road surfaces. Air-filled tires, however, generated a lot of unwanted "bounce for the ounce." To isolate passengers from this movement, different types of springs were developed.

Types of Front and Rear Suspensions

Each wheel is attached to the frame of the car by metal arms called **control arms**. The name of each is determined by its shape and its location (upper or lower). For example, A-arms are made in the triangular shape of the letter A. A wishbone is made in the shape of—surprise, surprise—a wishbone. A control arm may be upper, lower, or trailing (that is, it may trail behind the frame or cross member).

Springs compress to absorb the impact of wheels hitting a bump. When the car passes to level ground, they extend to release this motion. They act like the body's knees. Springs are attached to the car by combining them with arms and wishbones to give a smooth ride and to help the vehicle hold the road properly. The three main types of springs are coil springs, leaf springs, and torsion bars.

Coil springs, the most common ones in use today on passenger cars, look like oversized metal Slinkies as they compress and extend again and again (in response to the

Torsion bar

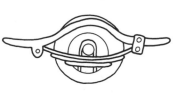

Leaf spring

**Coil springs
Double wishbone**

**Coil springs
Trailing arm**

irregularities in the road surface), before returning to their original shape. **Leaf springs** absorb the motion of the wheels as the uneven strips of metal of which they're made flatten and unflatten. They are still found on many four-wheel drive vehicles and in the rear of light trucks and some domestic passenger cars. **Torsion bars** absorb the road motion by means of a bar that twists and turns as the motion is received.

Like a door closure, the shock absorber absorbs the motion of the springs.

Shock Absorbers

Any type of spring would keep compressing and extending until we were begging for Dramamine if it weren't for shock absorbers, which work like a door closure, the kind with the metal tube that allows the door to open freely and close slowly. By absorbing some of the motion, the fluid in the door closure controls the speed at which the door returns to its original position. In a similar way, the shock absorber controls the up-and-down movement of the spring.

Like the door closure, the shock absorber is a sealed system filled with fluid; it contains two tubes that share a common center and a piston. The top of the shock absorber tube is attached to the frame of the car; the bottom is attached to a suspension arm. As the car moves up and down, the fluid is pushed through tiny openings, allowing the piston to move up and down faster or slower, depending on the size of the openings. This reduces the amount of up-and-down motion that is transferred to the passenger compartment (the smoothness or bumpiness of the ride).

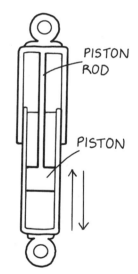

The shock absorber contains two tubes that share a common center and a piston.

Specialized Shock Absorbers

A variety of shock absorbers have been developed in recent years for the purpose of giving passengers the most comfortable ride, with the greatest control, and under a variety of different load conditions. Here are the main types.

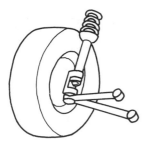

A MacPherson strut combines the spring and shock absorber into one unit.

MacPherson struts are one of a variety of specialized shock absorbers available on modern vehicles. They are particularly popular because they combine some of the traditional suspension components and eliminate others to make a smaller, lighter, more compact unit. They are found in almost all front-wheel drive vehicles and in the front of many rear-wheel drive vehicles as well.

MacPherson struts combine the spring and shock absorber into one unit. This design results in greater stability and improved road handling, which is why MacPherson struts are believed to be superior to many other suspensions in which the shock and the spring are separate.

Heavy-duty Shock Absorbers

Heavy-duty shocks are regular shock absorbers but larger in size and with more fluid. The more fluid, the more motion the shock absorber can absorb. A heavy-duty shock absorber can handle greater loads and keep the wheels planted firmly on the ground, but the ride is harsher. These replacement shock absorbers are worth considering if your car frequently tows heavy loads.

Frequently asked questions

Q How often should shock absorbers be replaced?

A Check your owner's manual for the manufacturer's recommendations, but keep in mind that it's a good idea to have your original shock absorbers and struts checked after 25,000 miles (40,500 kilometers), then every 15,000 miles (24,300 kilometers). Worn shocks or struts can increase wear and tear of your car's tires, suspension, and steering components.

After a heavy workout, any shock absorber is prone to "fading," becoming temporarily less efficient.

❖

Gas-powered Shock Absorbers

After a heavy workout, any shock absorber is prone to "fading." Fading occurs when a shock absorber works too hard, for example, riding on rough, unpaved roads. In response to this excessive demand, one tube moves rapidly and continuously inside the other, causing air bubbles to form inside the tubes. The shock absorber becomes temporarily less efficient and the quality of the ride is consequently diminished. Endless bouncing takes place even if the shocks are new. **Gas-powered shock absorbers** were developed as one response to this problem.

Gas-powered shock absorbers, which are becoming standard on many newer model cars, use a nitrogen charge to pressurize the fluid in the piston. Under pressure, air bubbles can't form. The shock absorbers maintain a steady performance, providing a smooth ride regardless of the difficulty or the unfriendliness of the terrain.

Variable Load Shock Absorber

If your car frequently carries dramatically different weights at different times, you might want to consider a

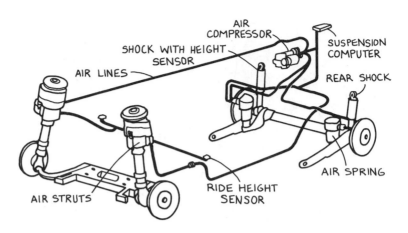

In an active suspension, a computer responds to many sensors that detect tiny changes in the movement of the vehicle's body and wheels.

❖

variable load shock absorber. Either mechanically or electronically (by computer), the shock absorber responds differently to various weights carried in the car. The variable load shock absorber does this by first sensing a change in weight. It then changes the size of the piston's openings: larger and the ride is smoother, smaller and the ride is harsher.

Ball Joints and Bushings

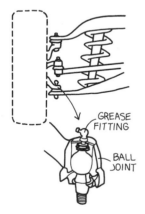

Ball joints are the connecting joints of the steering and suspension systems.

Ball joints are the connecting joints of the steering and suspension systems. An integral part of both the steering and the suspension, ball joints allow the steering components to move up and down, as well as side to side, compensating for uneven road surfaces. As ball joints wear, you might experience a "sloppiness" or feeling of looseness in the steering as you drive.

One other suspension part that you may eventually need to replace during the lifetime of your car is a bushing. This metal or rubber lining helps to reduce wear between two parts by acting as a cushion. Bushings are not restricted to the suspension but are found throughout the car.

Active or "Road Smart" Suspension

In active suspensions, a series of sensors feeds information about vehicle speed, braking, and other handling characteristics to a computer. The computer then adjusts the ride (by altering the spring and shock absorber movements) for changing road conditions, thus enhancing ride comfort and handling. Computers can even direct the suspension components to adjust the load on each wheel. This will help the car to lean to the inside when rounding a curve, like a motorcycle does. Who knows? Someday computers may enable cars to walk up stairs.

Some new cars have computer-assisted suspension components that allow the car to lean into the curve, somewhat like a motorcycle does.

It's Not Just Vanilla Anymore

Many of today's vehicles come with a variety of suspension choices, from a base system to off-road, from sport to touring. Each has its own distinctive comfort and handling characteristics. When looking at suspension features, first evaluate your own driving needs. Be sure you test drive a vehicle with the same suspension system that you will be buying. Test drive different types, but be sure that you really need the super-duper, more expensive suspension before you pay for it. If you're a speed-limit highway driver, you may be buying features that you will never take advantage of.

Suspension System Choices

Making your car go the distance

Steering and Suspension Systems

Here are some tips to keep these systems in good working order.

✓ Check the power steering fluid level in the reservoir or have it checked about once a month, and top it off when necessary. The dipstick is usually located under the cap of the power steering pump.

✓ If you have to add fluid every time you check the dipstick, there's probably a leak in the system. Have it inspected by a professional.

✓ When adding fluid, check your owner's manual for the correct type. Power steering and automatic transmission fluids are not interchangeable, and substitutions can cause serious problems.

✓ Have the suspension and steering components inspected and adjusted at manufacturer's recom-

Money-Saving Tip

"Front end work," a term that lumps together all repairs on the steering and suspension components, has traditionally been an area of high consumer dissatisfaction. If a technician recommends the replacement of steering or suspension components, ask the shop to show you what method is being used to determine wear. Often it is the manufacturer's specifications (tolerances) that determine excess wear, not the earlier method of shaking or moving a component. For this precise diagnosis a technician needs a sophisticated dial-indicator gauge.

mended intervals. The rods, levers, and connectors wear with use and stretch with age. Proper inspection and adjustment will extend their useful life by many thousands of miles.

✓ Watch for signs of shock absorber wear, which can be detected by stepping down on one side of the bumper and then releasing it. If the car continues to bounce up and down more than three times, you probably have a worn shock absorber.

✓ Some steering and suspension components are quick and easy to reach; others are not. Make sure your estimate indicates parts and labor costs, and then check around to see if the quoted price is reasonable

Regularly check the power steering fluid level in the reservoir.

More bounce than usual   **Car dips forward when braking**

Noise and bottoming out on bumps   **Dark fluid on shock absorber**

Signs of Shock Absorber Wear

Troubleshooting the Steering and Suspension Systems

Possible causes →

Symptoms	Low power steering fluid	Slipping power steering belt	Faulty power steering pump	Wheel bearings	Worn/loose steering component/linkage	Lack of suspension/steering lubrication	Worn/loose suspension components (suspension arms/ball joints)	Worn shock absorbers, struts, bushings	Loose nuts and bolts in steering/suspension	Worn/broken springs	Wheels out of alignment
Car pulls to one side				●	●		●		●	●	●
Car hard to steer	●	●	●		●		●		●		
Looseness in steering					●				●		
Car vibrates at high speeds					●			●	●		●
Steering wheel shakes					●		●	●	●		
Growling noise	●		●	●							
Loud squealing noise		●									
Noises (thumps) in front end					●	●	●		●	●	
Body sways excessively in corners					●		●			●	
Car wanders over road					●	●	●	●		●	●

*Be certain to check tires and air pressure in tires before repairs to the suspension system are attempted.

13
BRAKES

Brakes play a critical role in your safety. In this chapter you'll learn how brakes work, why they sometimes squeak and squeal, and whether you should be concerned if yours do. You'll learn what to look for if your brakes are about to let you down, and how you can avoid expensive brake component replacement with timely brake maintenance. Also covered are how antilock brakes and traction control work.

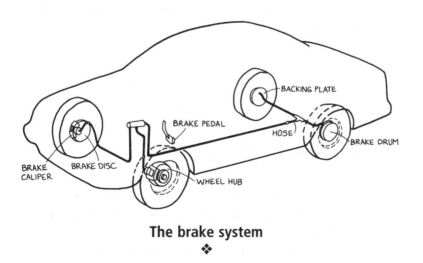

The brake system

❖

Early cars had brakes only on the rear wheels. The systems were often inefficient, complex, and, not infrequently, hazardous to one's health. Brakes often experienced "**fading**," a terrifying condition in which the brakes failed completely as a result of overheating. Early

Getting a ton or more of metal and rubber to roar down the road is only half the battle; prudence dictates that we also have a reliable way to stop it.

❖

BRAKES WORK ON THE PRINCIPLE THAT FLUIDS RESIST Being COMPRESSED

brakes also required a lot of strength from the driver to stop the car.

How Brakes Work

Brake systems operate on all four wheels of the car and use brake fluid under pressure to stop the car when you step on the brake pedal.

Today's vehicles have a dual braking system; the front and the rear brakes operate separately. Here are the steps and components:

Brake fluid is stored in a metal or plastic container called a **master cylinder**, which is divided into two sections. Each section activates a separate set of brakes. If

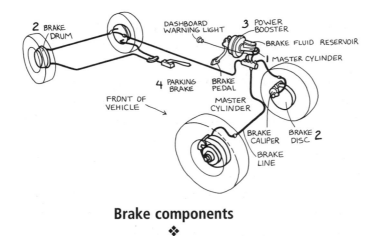

Brake components
❖

there is a leak in either one of the systems, a valve seals off the malfunctioning system from the healthy system. This is to ensure that you will always be able to stop the car.

When you push on the brake pedal, brake fluid is forced out of the master cylinder through the **brake lines** to the brakes at each wheel.

The two types of brakes are **disc brakes** and **drum brakes**. Disc brakes are generally found in the front of a vehicle (where most of the braking is done), and drum brakes in the rear. Today, however, many vehicles have four-wheel disc brakes.

Power brakes use the power of the engine to assist braking. The power brake booster adds pressure to the brake fluid so that you don't need to exert as much pressure.

On most cars, the parking, or emergency, brake works on the rear brakes. When the parking brake is applied, the brake linings are forced against the drums until released. This keeps the car from moving after it has already stopped.

Drum Brakes

In a drum brake, a round metal container is attached to the turning wheel. Inside are two crescent-shaped pieces of metal called **brake shoes**. The shoes are backed with

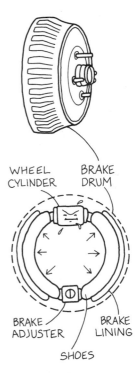

In a drum brake a round metal container is attached to the turning wheel. Inside are two crescent-shaped objects called brake shoes.

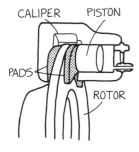

With disc brakes, a pair of kidney-shaped brake pads backed with friction material sits on either side of a metal disc called a rotor. The rotor is connected to the turning wheel.

friction material called **brake linings**. The composition of this friction material is similar to that of a clutch disc: tough and heat-resistant.

Between the two linings is a hollow tube called a **wheel cylinder**. Inside the wheel cylinder are two arms, called pistons. When you push on the brake pedal, brake fluid is forced through the brake lines and fills the wheel cylinder to capacity. This forces the pistons out against the linings, and the linings now rub against the inside of the drum. The resulting friction causes the drum and the wheel to slow down and eventually to stop. When the brake pedal is released, the fluid returns to the reservoir, and return springs bring the shoes back into their original positions. The shoes remain in this retracted position until the pedal is pushed again.

Disc Brakes

Disc brakes use the same principle as drum brakes but different mechanisms. A pair of kidney-shaped brake pads lined with friction material sit on either side of a metal disc called a **rotor**. The rotor is connected to the turning wheel. A **caliper**, a metal "fist" with one or two pistons in it, is attached to the brake pads. When you step on the brake pedal, the brake fluid is forced out of the master cylinder to the caliper. In the caliper, the brake fluid forces the pistons to squeeze the pads against the turning rotor. This causes the rotor and the wheel to slow and eventually stop.

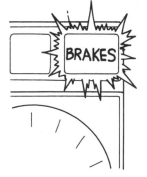

Brake warning light

Brake Warning Light

If a brake warning light flashes on the instrument panel even occasionally, it indicates trouble in the system. You could have a loss of brake fluid, a leak in the brake system, or air in the brake lines. Or it may simply mean that your rear or parking brakes need adjustment. Get the vehicle slowly and safely off the road, and have the system inspected by a professional as soon as possible. And

Money-Saving Tip

Have brake fluid changed every two or three years, or every 30,000 miles, whichever comes first. Brake fluid is subject to contamination by moisture, which can enter through the rubber brake lines that carry it. This caustic fluid deteriorates with age. When it does, it attacks the expensive brake components. Periodically replacing brake fluid will save you expensive brake component replacement in the future.

always double-check to make certain you have fully released the parking brake before attempting to drive off.

Early Warning System

You may hear a chirping noise coming from the front wheels, not when you're braking, but when the car is moving. If so, it is probably a "brake wear indicator" or sensor, a small piece of soft metal positioned so that it touches the surface of the rotor when the pad is ready to be replaced. It's saying, "Hey there! Your brake pads are low. Replace them now, before a routine maintenance item like brake pad replacement develops into the expensive replacement of major brake components!"

Antilock Brakes

Antilock brake systems (ABS) have been around since the late 1940s, but until recently, they weren't installed

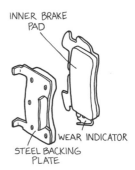

INNER BRAKE PAD

WEAR INDICATOR

STEEL BACKING PLATE

A brake wear indicator makes a high-pitched warning sound when the brake pads need replacement.

Stopping a car quickly requires good traction.

❖

on anything you would have driven—unless you were a licensed commercial pilot. This computer-controlled automatic braking system helps you to steer around an obstacle while braking hard, even on slick surfaces.

To understand how antilock brakes work, it's important to remember that the reason a moving car sticks to the road is because the car's tires turn. The turning of the tires against the road surface generates friction. We call that friction **traction**.

Now imagine that a child's ball rolls out in front of a moving car. How do most people respond? They stomp on the brake pedal. And what very often happens? The car skids because the brakes are applied with such force that they stop the tires from turning. This is called "wheel lock-up." No turning, no friction. No friction, no traction.

Now, traction's a good thing. (Unless, of course, you've been in an accident; that kind of traction is no fun.) Without traction, your one-ton-plus hunk of metal and rubber thinks it's parked.

The purpose of an antilock braking system is to avoid wheel lock-up and to allow the driver to maintain control. A computer receives messages from sensors located at the wheels. If a wheel is about to lock up, the computer automatically reduces the braking force at that wheel and then reapplies it when the wheel starts to turn again. The effect is similar to pumping the brakes, but at a rate much faster than most drivers ever could achieve. It's like having Mario Andretti driving your car for you at that moment. The car will not necessarily stop any quicker, but stability and steering control are maintained.

The correct way to use ABS in an emergency is to step on the brake pedal hard and continue to steer around obstacles. You will probably sense the brake pedal vibrate and you may hear noises, or a dash light may indicate the ABS system has been activated. By the way, all ABS systems are designed so that the car will have normal (non-ABS assisted) braking should the ABS system fail.

Stomp and Steer

During emergency braking, if your vehicle is equipped with antilock brakes, remember "stomp and steer": push down hard on the brake pedal and keep it depressed while continuing to steer.

Traction Control

Traction control is an adjunct to ABS that uses sophisticated electronics to help you stay on track even when the

◀ No ABS

◀ With ABS

Antilock brakes help you avoid wheel lock-up and allow you to maintain control of your vehicle.

Frequently asked questions

Q I just got new brakes, and they squeak. I asked about this and the repair shop said it's normal. Are they telling me the truth?

A Probably, but the condition isn't "normal," it's "common." Modern brake pads and linings are no longer made of asbestos (thanks to the EPA), but of tiny slivers of metal and other materials compressed together. These brake pads and linings are much harder than asbestos. They have excellent friction qualities, but, unfortunately, they often make noise.

The trick is to determine whether the noise is a problem or just an annoyance. Sometimes the sounds are the result of tiny variations in the surface of the pad. The newer type pads often don't conform as easily to the surface of the rotor. A squeak or squeal may be the result of vibrations. If you've had a new set of brake pads installed and are hearing this sound, have the brake work re-checked by the shop that did the work. They should be looking for loose parts.

Changes in temperature or changes in the moisture content of the atmosphere also affect friction characteristics that can set off a round of squeaking and squealing.

road is slick. A computer tracks input from wheel sensors that feed back information about the movement of the wheels. If the computer receives information that a wheel is about to slip, it automatically applies brakes to the problem wheel. It may also reduce engine power and make a change to the transmission gearing. Wheel slippage is eliminated, traction is restored, and the vehicle retains its grip.

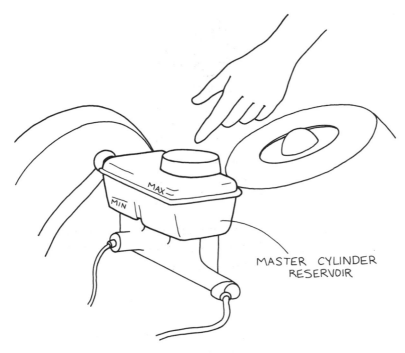

Check the brake fluid level in the master cylinder reservoir once a month, or have a professional check it for you.

Making your car go the distance

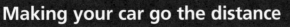

Brake System

Here are some tips to help ensure that your brakes are responsive and reliable.

✓ Check or have the brake fluid level in the master cylinder reservoir checked once a month. Most cars have a translucent brake fluid reservoir that allows you to check the fluid level without opening the container. If the brake fluid is low on a regular basis, have the system professionally inspected as soon as possible.

✓ If you have to add brake fluid, wipe the top of the container with a clean cloth before opening.

A thorough brake inspection includes examination of the master cylinder, the brake lines, linings, rotors, drums, pads, calipers, and wheel cylinders.

❖

Contaminated brake fluid has been responsible for more than one instance of brake failure.

✓ Learn to recognize the signs of faulty brakes: brake noise (such as squeaking or grinding), a low or spongy feel to the brake pedal, rapid brake fluid loss, or a pulsating or vibrating brake pedal. Note: If you notice the brake fluid is disappearing on a regular basis, have the system professionally inspected as soon as possible.

✓ Have a professional check the brake system once a year. The technician should inspect all working parts and report what percentage of your brake pads and linings remain. They should be replaced when they still have about 25 to 30 percent of their friction material. Excess wear ruins rotors and drums, which greatly reduces braking efficiency and dramatically adds to repair costs.

✓ Brake pads and linings are "normal wear and tear" items. As the brake pads and linings get thinner, they have to travel farther to make contact with the rotor or drum, and braking action gradually diminishes. A periodic brake adjustment is often required to compensate on drum brakes. Disc brakes are self-adjusting.

Squeaking or grinding can indicate worn brakes.

✓ Be sure your regular brake service includes a parking brake inspection and adjustment when necessary. If the parking brake is working correctly, the car should not move forward easily in drive or first gear.

✓ Replace brake pads and linings with materials similar to the original equipment: have semi-metallic pads replaced with semi-metallic and non-metallic replaced with non-metallic. An occasional squeak or squeal that does not affect good braking is probably something you'll have to live with. *Note:* Have brakes inspected immediately if there is any change in the braking pattern.

✓ Brake service often includes shaving off a thin layer of metal from the rotor or drum to remove scratches and irregularities in their surface. This process is called **cutting** or **turning**, and there is a legal limit to how much metal can be removed. If the scratches or grooves are too deep, you may need to buy new rotors or drums. Brake components, no matter what kind, are always replaced in pairs.

✓ Ask for a written warranty or guarantee and read it over carefully. Ask questions about anything you do not fully understand.

✓ Wheel bearings are usually serviced when brake work is done. In some vehicles, wheel bearings are removed periodically and repacked with clean grease to extend the life of the working parts.

On most front-wheel-drive vehicles, front wheel bearings are sealed at the factory. If they wear, they must be replaced, and they are always replaced in pairs. Read your owner's manual for specifics.

Troubleshooting the Brake System

Symptoms \ Possible causes	Air in brake fluid	Low/contaminated brake fluid	Worn/glazed pads/linings	Grease/fluid on pads/linings	Pads/linings need adjustment	Defective master cylinder	Defective wheel cylinder/caliper	Faulty power brake booster	Warped brake disc/drum	Dirt in brake mechanism	Clogged/kinked/weak hoses and lines	Parking brake adjustment/rust	Computer-related (ABS)
Brake warning light on		●			●	●					●	●	
Pedal hard (excess pedal effort)			●	●		●	●	●		●			
Pedal spongy	●					●							
Pedal sinks to floor	●			●	●	●							
Pedal vibrates/pulsates	●								●				
Noise when brakes applied			●		●				●	●			●
Brakes grab			●	●									
Brakes pull	●		●	●		●	●			●			
Brakes drag			●		●				●	●			
Parking brake inoperative												●	
ABS light on													●

14
TIRES, WHEELS, AND OTHER ROUND THINGS

Your tires are the only direct contact your car has with the road. This chapter shows what you can do to make them perform better and last longer, including how to buy the right tires for your car at the best price. It also explains what wheel balancing, alignment, and rotation are and when they should be done.

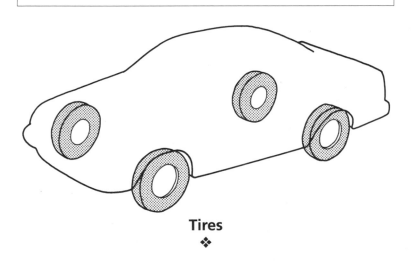

Tires

❖

In combination with your car's suspension, steering, and brakes, tires help to keep your car on the road and going in the direction you want. Four contact patches that are no bigger than the size of your hand are the only connection between your car and the road. Tires also provide a nice pillow of air in the form of a spongy rubber shoe worn by your car's metal feet, the wheels.

Today's tires are constructed of a combination of fabrics and materials that isolate you from the jolting impact of the bumps, stones, potholes, and washboard surfaces over which you travel. They are designed to provide a compromise between comfort, good road handling, and long wear. Their predecessors, on the other hand, endlessly jiggled and jostled their passenger's spines and dentures and were, according to many accounts, one of the most expensive and least reliable of all car parts. Deeply rutted roads filled with nails left by decades of horseshoes made two and three punctures on a journey commonplace. For many years, tires were drivers' weakest link.

In the early days, cars ran on tires of narrow solid rubber, and the ride was uncomfortable and unstable. It was common to see cars in ditches along the side of the road. A car was about as predictable as a skittish horse, and it would be a while before the term "steady as she goes" could accurately be applied to automobiles.

As cars grew larger and heavier and engine speeds increased, they needed greater stability in the form of a bigger, broader footprint. Tire manufacturers responded with the development of wider balloon tires. The chances of a car's staying on the road improved dramatically. The chances improved even more with the addition of "grooves"—channels cut in the smooth rubber of the tread (the part that comes in contact with the road).

How Tires Work

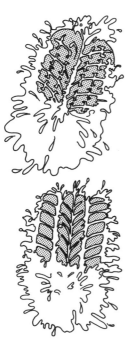

Grooves are channels cut into the tire. They provide drainage for water.

Theoretically, the best design for a tire would be a wide smooth one, with no grooves or indentations. This design would provide the maximum surface for contacting the road. If grooves are made in this smooth surface, the amount of tire surface in direct contact with the road is reduced. But the grooves provide drainage for water, mud, and snow so that secure contact with the road can be maintained. Smooth or grooved tires? The answer is both. And the compromise between the two dictates the construction of every modern tire.

Mr. Goodyear perfected his tire by mistake.

❖

Early Tire Development

Tires owe a debt to Mrs. Goodyear. Her husband, Charles, experimented with tire-making for more than five years. His obsession led his family to public ridicule, poverty, and to debtor's prison. He finally promised his wife that he would give up his quest. But in a weak moment, while Mrs. Goodyear was away from home, he broke his word and began experimenting with one element he had not tried before. Unfortunately, or fortunately as it turned out, Mrs. Goodyear returned home unexpectedly. Goodyear threw the mixture in the oven to avoid detection. Sometime later he retrieved his concoction and discovered that heat had been just the thing it needed. His kitchen experiment would eventually produce the material that would be the foundation for modern tires, a solid substance with plenty of give: rubber.

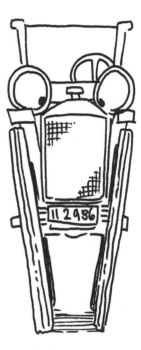

In 1900, the average family traveled about 200 miles a year. Today's family travels about 15,000.

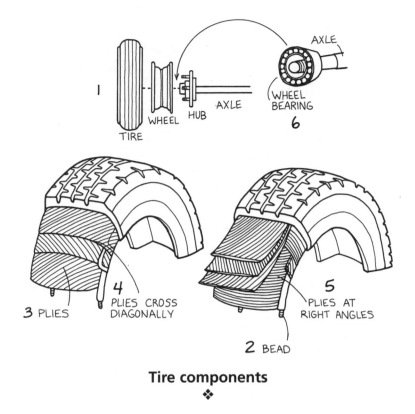

Tire components

❖

You've Come a Long Way, Baby

Great advances have been made in tire construction since Mr. Goodyear's domestic experiments. Here are the basic components of today's tires:

Steel wheels are attached to the hubs located at the end of each axle by heavy metal bolts called lugs. The lugs are secured by lug nuts.

A **bead**, thin strips of metal wound together into a narrow ring, provides an airtight grip on the wheels.

Plies are pieces of material that are attached to the bead. It is the material of the ply and the angle at which the threads or "cords" of the plies meet each other that determine the tire's construction category.

Bias-ply tires have plies that meet each other on the diagonal. In other words, at an angle of roughly 35 to 40 degrees.

Radial tires, which are standard equipment on most newer cars, have plies that meet each other at right angles, that is, 90 degrees. Radials provide a more comfortable ride and contain strips of metal or fiberglass which make the tires stiffer, improve their cornering capability, and extend their useful life.

Wheel bearings are metal doughnuts with many tiny steel balls, called ball bearings, inside. They extend the life of the axles and contribute significantly to proper road handling through smooth steering and braking. They distribute the weight and turning force of the axle shaft. They are found where the axle joins the wheel.

Reading Tires

In order to help consumers choose from the numerous tire models that are available, the government has developed a uniform rating system that includes three categories: traction, resistance to heat, and resistance to wear. This rating is stamped on the side of all passenger car tires (not truck or snow tires), along with symbols that indicate the tire's size and type of construction. The illustration on the following page shows you how to interpret this information and can help you choose a quality product and correct replacement tire for your car.

1. **a & b.** The brand name and tire model.
2. Tire's type of construction.
3. Maximum Air Pressure. This is *not* the recommended inflation pressure for your tires. That number is specific to your vehicle. See below for more about tire pressure.
4. DOT and the letters and numbers following are the tire's identification number, useful if the tire is recalled. The last three digits, 035, indicate the week and the last digit of the year the tire was made. This tire was manufactured in the third week of 1995. When buying tires, look for those tires that have been manufactured within the last year.
5. Tire size and general type.
   a. P stands for passenger vehicle.
   b. The number 195 tells you how wide the tire is. It's measured in millimeters.

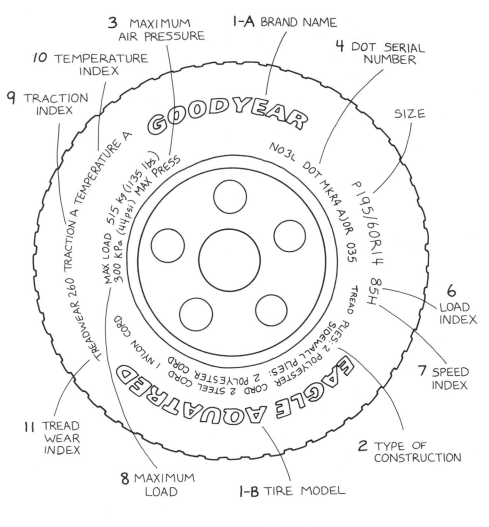

Rating and reading tires

❖

c. The number 60 indicates how tall the tire is. It is represented as a ratio of the tire's height divided by its width. The tires with taller sidewalls (ratios of 60 or 70) are often found on passenger cars. Tires with shorter sidewalls (ratios of 50) are more often found on sports cars and are called performance tires. They offer improved steering response and road feel. The drawback is that passengers often experience a harsher ride.

    d. The letter R indicates the way in which the tire is constructed. R stands for radial ply. All new passenger cars and light trucks are equipped with radials, and most replacement tires are radials.

    e. The number 14 indicates the wheel diameter this tire fits, as measured in inches.

6. The load index indicates the maximum weight that this tire can carry at its maximum speed rating.

7. The letter H indicates the tire's speed rating. H indicates a speed rating up to 130 mph (210 km/h). The top ratings are W which indicates a speed rating of 168 mph (269 km/h), and Z which has an unlimited speed rating.

8. "Tread wear" rates how long a tire is expected to last. Ratings start at 100 and go up to 500. In general, a tire with a 200 rating will last twice as long as a tire with a 100.

    It's important to remember that tire wear is also determined by tire maintenance (inflation) and how you drive. High-speed driving causes more heat and thus, more wear. Where you drive is also a factor (substandard roads take their toll on rubber).

9. "Traction" followed by a letter grade of A to C, rates the tire's ability to stop on a wet road surface. C is the lowest measure. The important word here is wet. This index does not reveal the tire's capabilities on a dry pavement or any other type of surface. While it is important, it should not be the only factor influencing a buying decision.

10. "Temperature" grades the tire's ability to withstand and dissipate heat. A is the highest grade; C is the lowest.

All-Season Versus Mud and Snow Tires

Conventional treads provide good traction on dry roads. All-season tires last longer than snow tires and still do a reasonably good job of handling bad weather

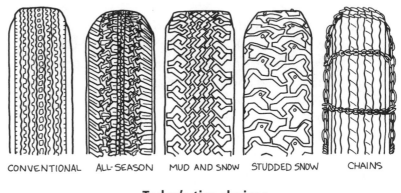

CONVENTIONAL   ALL-SEASON   MUD AND SNOW   STUDDED SNOW   CHAINS

Today's tire choices
❖

road conditions. If you live in an area where the average snow and ice accumulation is marginal, all-season tires can save you some money by limiting you to one set of tires.

The tread on a mud and snow tire has especially deep grooves, which are specifically designed to dig down and make contact with the road surface below. This aggressive tread works great on ice and snow, but it wears faster on dry roads than a conventional tread does.

Studded tires have metal studs embedded in them. While not legal in all states, they offer even more traction in the toughest of conditions.

Money-Saving Tip

 Research tells us that as many as half the cars on the road have at least one tire that is seriously underinflated. That's bad news, since the single largest reason for tire failure (blowouts) is underinflation. Furthermore, underinflated tires do not handle as well, take longer to stop, and wear faster. Even a small degree (4 psi) of underinflation can decrease a tire's life by as much as 10 percent. Checking tire pressure can protect both your safety and your pocketbook.

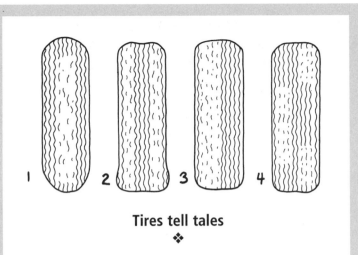

Tires tell tales

❖

1. Overinflation—When a tire has too much air (is overinflated), only its middle section touches the road surface. The tire's sides pull up and away from the road and only a small amount of tread makes contact with the road. There is excessive wear in the middle.

2. Underinflation—When a tire does not have enough air (is underinflated), its sides sag and puff out, and its middle section pulls up and away from the pavement. Only a small portion of the tread makes contact with the road. The tire will show wear on the edges.

3. Tread wear on one side only—An irregular tread wear pattern on the tire, with wear accelerated on one side only, is often an indicator of alignment problems.

4. Tire is worn erratically—If the tire is worn erratically (a pattern that is referred to as cupping, or scalloping) it may be that the wheel is out of balance, or the shock absorbers or ball joints may be worn.

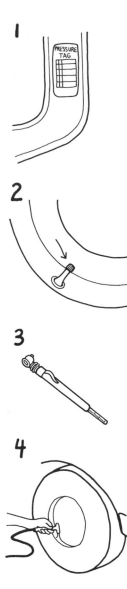

Checking tire pressure is easy.

Chains may also be an option if you live in an area where you get heavy snow, but only occasionally. They cannot be driven at highway speeds on dry roads. Although chains are easier to install than they were years ago, putting chains on still means getting out of the car in the snow and crawling around on your hands and knees.

Special Spare Tires

Small or "doughnut" spare tires are good at doing what they're designed for, that is, saving storage space. They are to be driven at a speed no greater than the number stamped on the side of the tire and must be replaced with a standard spare as soon as possible. As an added bonus, you don't have to be Man Mountain Dean to get it out of the trunk if you do have to change a flat tire.

Run-flat Tires

Run-flat tires can be driven for limited distances even while deflated. They have been specially reinforced to retain their shape and support a vehicle's weight so that the driver retains full control, even with the tire at zero pressure.

Making your car go the distance

Tire and Wheels

✓ Check tire pressure once a month and before going on a trip. Don't forget to check the spare—even spares can lose air. And don't assume that the air pressure in your tires is correct because they look okay.

✓ Use a good quality tire gauge. Tire gauges come in two basic types: pencil and dial. The dial gauges cost more, but they are a little easier to read. Just be sure the one you buy can measure inflation up to 60 pounds since the smaller spare tires usually need this higher pressure.

✓ Check tires when they are cold, i.e., the car should be standing for a few hours before you check them. As you drive, the tire temperature rises and so does the pressure. Warm tires will give an inaccurate reading. Follow these steps:

1. Locate the automaker's recommended tire pressure for your car. Ignore the number printed on the tire; it is generally too high for normal use. Look in the glove compartment or inside one of the door jambs for a label with the words "Cold Tire Pressure" followed by the letters "F" for front and "R" for rear.

2. Locate the valve stem on the tire and remove its protective cap.

3. Apply the tire gauge to the valve stem at a right angle and push firmly. If using a pencil-type gauge, be sure to push the nylon measurement tab all the way in before applying it to the valve stem. You will probably hear a whoosh of air, which is normal. (You are not letting all the air out of your tires—unless you continue to push on the pin, in which case air will escape.) The firmer and more directly you apply the gauge, the less air will leak out. The nylon tab will pop out of the bottom of the gauge, revealing a number that indicates the air pressure in pounds per square inch. If you're using a dial type, the needle will move from zero to a number.

4. If your pressure is too low, drive to a nearby service station to add air. Do not trust the service station's gauge; most are notoriously inaccurate. That's why you have your own gauge.

Checking Tread Wear

Check tread wear with an inexpensive tread depth indicator or an even less expensive penny. Replace tires when the tread has worn to approximately $\frac{1}{16}$ inch (1.6 mm). Don't wait until you need an immediate replacement.

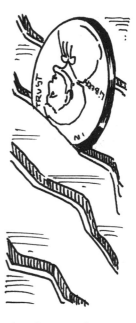

Check tread depth by sticking a penny in a groove. If you can see the top of Abe's head (or all of the Queen's crown), it's time for a new set of tires.

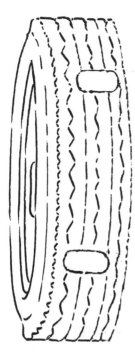

Today's tires sport indicators called wear bars.

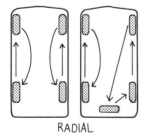

RADIAL

You'll find the tire rotation pattern for your car in your owner's manual. Here is one common pattern.

You increase the risk of tire failure and may miss out on buying the best quality tires on sale.

✓ Today's tires also have wear indicators in them called **wear bars**. A wear bar is a thin bald strip that appears across two or more treads when the tread has worn to about a ¹⁄₁₆ inch (1.6 mm) depth. Keep an eye out for these and when they appear, begin looking for replacement tires.

✓ Watch for tears, bulges, or abnormal lumps in the tread or sidewall. If you find any of these defects, have the tire checked immediately and replaced, if necessary.

✓ To ensure longer life and even wear, tires should be rotated every 8,000 miles (13,000 kilometers). Front tires typically wear faster than rear ones, because the weight in the car shifts forward when you stop. Front wheels also feel the impact of steering, and in the case of front-wheel drive, driving.

✓ If you switch to snow or alternate tires during the year, make sure the tires are marked as they are removed from the car. Their position on the car should be written on the tire with chalk or an easily readable, non-permanent marker.

Wheel Alignment

Alignment has to do with the angle at which the tires meet the road. For a car to handle well, the tires need to sit slightly tilted to the road surface. It takes a trained technician with a computerized alignment machine to create an angle that best accommodates these needs.

✓ To ensure longer tire life, have a wheel alignment check whenever your tires are being serviced. If there is a deviation from manufacturer specifications, corrections are made to the camber (the inward or out-

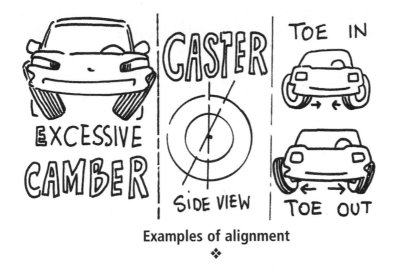

Examples of alignment

❖

ward tilt of a wheel), caster (the forward or rearward tilt of a wheel when viewed from the side), and toe (a measure of two wheels' parallel alignment; "**toe in**" is analogous to a pigeon-toed condition, and "**toe out**" is analogous to a duck-footed condition).

  The frequency of a wheel alignment check depends on the type of driving you do and the road conditions, but once a year is a good rule of thumb. Rough roads, gravity force starts, quarter horse stops, and parking on the curb instead of next to it will increase your need for more frequent alignment.

  Most cars today (all those with independent rear suspensions) require an alignment of all four wheels. If a technician speaks about a front-wheel alignment, be wary. If you are uncertain what type of rear suspension your vehicle has, ask your regular service provider.

  A good alignment technician always checks for worn steering and suspension parts and for dragging brakes before doing an alignment.

  Make certain your tires are properly inflated before having them aligned.

Frequently asked questions

Q What really happens when a car hydroplanes?

A **Hydroplaning** is a scary driving condition that occurs when a layer of water forms between the tire and the road surface. The treads cannot push the water through fast enough. The tire climbs up on a wedge of water and suddenly looses contact with the road. Traction and control go right out the window. Tire grooves can push only so much water through them before they fill. Sufficient tread, the correct tire pressure, and slowing your car's speed as you approach large puddles helps the vehicle regain traction by allowing the grooves more time to work.

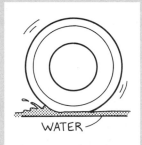

WATER

Hydroplaning occurs when a layer of water forms between the tire and the road surface.

✓ Make certain each wheel alignment check and any required adjustments are noted on the repair order. There may only be two checks done if the caster was pre-set by the manufacturer. Ask that each adjustment be explained to you.

If no corrections are needed after an alignment inspection, the charge is generally less than that for inspecting and making adjustments.

✓ To avoid warped rotors, insist that a torque wrench be used to tighten all lug nuts and that the wrench be set to manufacturer's specifications.

Wheel Balancing

Wheel balancing compensates for a tire's unevenness (they look round but they're not). Small metal weights are attached to the wheels to make them turn evenly. There are two popular ways to balance tires—static, with the wheels off the car, and dynamic, with the wheels on. The preferred method is dynamic balancing because it allows for the influence of the brakes and suspension components.

✓ Have your wheels balanced whenever having new tires mounted or whenever tires are removed from their rims. If you remove a tire simply to look at something else, the weights remain untouched, and the tire shouldn't need to be balanced.

✓ Wheel bearings are packed with grease, providing a lubricating cushion. Have wheel bearings repacked whenever your owner's manual suggests, or more frequently if you do a lot of off-road driving. Wheel bearings that are sealed at the factory should be replaced in pairs if they fail.

Replacing Tires

✓ Replacement tires should be the same size, design, and whenever possible, brand as the original tires.

✓ When buying replacement tires, take the time to learn more about them. Don't pay for tire qualities that you won't use.

✓ Make certain the price quoted for replacement tires includes wheel balancing and installation.

✓ Buying new tires does not necessarily mean that you need a wheel alignment. If the old tires were wearing uniformly, it's likely the new ones will also.

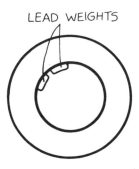

LEAD WEIGHTS

When wheels are balanced, small metal weights are attached to them to make the wheels turn evenly.

✓ Ask about written warranties before you buy. The longer, the better. And keep all documentation in a safe place.

Tire and Wheel Runout

Among the ills a tire or a wheel may suffer is **radial** or **lateral runout**. Radial runout is the difference between the low and high points on the tread of the tire. Lateral runout is the wobble of the tire or wheel. Both irregularities can be determined with a runout gauge and matched against manufacturer's specifications. If the runout is excessive, the remedy may be as simple as cleaning and remounting the tire. If that doesn't solve the problem, the tire and/or wheel should be replaced.

Troubleshooting Tires and Wheels

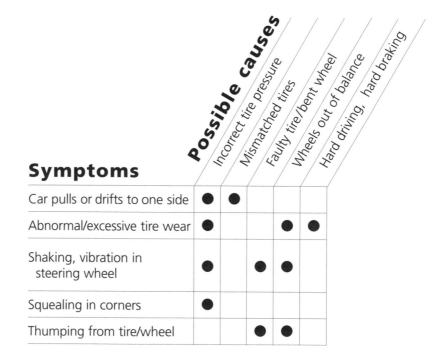

Symptoms	Incorrect tire pressure	Mismatched tires	Faulty tire/bent wheel	Wheels out of balance	Hard driving, hard braking
Car pulls or drifts to one side	●	●			
Abnormal/excessive tire wear	●			●	●
Shaking, vibration in steering wheel	●		●	●	
Squealing in corners	●				
Thumping from tire/wheel			●	●	

15
CHOOSING AND DEALING WITH SERVICE PROVIDERS

This chapter will help you to choose an honest and competent repair shop, and give you tips on how to deal with repair personnel. It will also teach you how to protect yourself against dishonesty, incompetence, and overcharging. You'll learn how to describe a symptom so that you have a better chance of getting the repair done right the first time. You'll also learn what you can do if it isn't right the first time.

You probably won't find yourself a fairy god-mechanic, but you can find honest, competent service professionals.

Do some research before you choose a repair shop.

Wouldn't it be wonderful if every time your car broke down, a fairy god-mechanic appeared and, with a wave of her magic ratchet, turned your lemon into a dream car? Unfortunately, mechanics in the real world are of the mere mortal variety. If you own a car, sooner or later you are going to have to pick one to work on it.

Choosing a repair shop is a task most consumers approach with all the fear, loathing, and paranoia they can muster. It doesn't have to be that way. The repair shops of this world are not all out to get us. But just as in any other profession, their ranks include the good, the bad, and the indifferent.

To be sure, there are a number of incompetent and unskilled technicians. In many states, all those with a rusty screwdriver and the inclination can call themselves technicians and offer to operate on your car. For the few states that do require certification or licensing of technicians, the requirements to qualify are usually minimal. As cars become more sophisticated, the situation worsens.

To complicate matters further, there are some in the field who, although they are skilled, lack scruples. Nevertheless, it's important that we don't lump all auto repair personnel in the same category. There are still a lot of technicians who are skilled and honest, and it is possible for you to find one. You don't even need a degree in auto repair, just common sense and the willingness to do some detective work.

Word of Mouth

When stalking a good repair shop, word of mouth is probably the best method. Ask your friends, relatives, co-workers, and insurance agents where they take their cars for servicing. Finding a qualified and honest technician can be just that easy. Use your common sense before acting on their recommendations. Just because Uncle Joe tells you he got a real good deal from See-U-Soon Auto Repair when they changed the oil in his car, it doesn't mean you should rush right down there and have your ailing transmission fixed. Even though the technicians at See-U-Soon may be wizards at changing oil, it could be that they wouldn't know a transmission if it crashed through the roof and landed with a bang in the garage bay.

Ask questions. What kind of work was done on Uncle Joe's car? Did the repair shop do just the work requested or did they make additional repairs? Did they exceed the estimate? If so, was there a valid reason and was Joe notified first? Is Uncle Joe known for his good judgment, or does he own 50 acres of swamp land in Florida? These are some of the questions that will get you the answers you need to make an intelligent decision.

Don't make the common mistake of restricting your choice to those shops closest to your home. A shop within walking distance is a great convenience, but should your car break down because Near-Your-House Fix-It didn't do the job right, you could find yourself a long, long way from home.

Other Methods

Although personal referral is one of the best ways to find a good technician, it is not the only way. There are other sources of this information. Automobile clubs, in addition to providing emergency road service, are also knowledgeable about good repair shops in your area. They often have lists which identify auto repair facilities that meet their standards of consistent, high-quality repair work and service. Consult your phone book. Shops with auto club approval usually mention that fact in their ads. Or call the auto clubs in your area for information.

Check the Shop's Reputation

Before you take your car into a new shop, don't forget to call the Consumer Complaint Division of your attorney general's office or the Better Business Bureau in your area. They won't recommend a technician or shop, but they will tell you if the one you're considering has unresolved complaints filed against it.

Today's cars require sophisticated diagnostic equipment to make repairs and to perform scheduled service properly.

❖

Don't Wait

It's best not to wait until you are in the vulnerable position of needing major repair work to try out a new shop or technician. Bring the car in first for a minor repair or routine maintenance job, such as an oil change or tire rotation. On that first visit, give the service area the "once over." Is it reasonably organized and clean? Or does it look like it's been stirred with a large spoon? Does it have computerized diagnostic tools? Or is the technician equipped with a large wrench, a rusty screwdriver, and little else?

Black Box Magic

"Black boxes," which run everything from computerized ignitions to air temperature control, have replaced many mechanical parts. A shop doesn't have to look like a hangar out of *Star Wars*, but it must have the manuals and equipment needed to work on your computerized car. At a minimum, it must have modern engine analyzing equipment. These diagnostic computers check major engine components and their functions. They then give a printout that indicates whether each system is working properly, pinpointing what is wrong, or what needs further examination. A good shop should be willing to discuss its equipment and show you how it works. Keep in mind that even the most sophisticated diagnostic equipment needs a properly trained technician to run it.

While some of the smaller shops do great work, they can't afford the computerized machines necessary for more complex technical repairs and adjustments. They may be forced to begin blindly switching parts until they stumble onto the right one.

Intermittent Problems

One of the most frustrating consequences of computerized cars occurs when the problem symptom happens only occasionally or disappears when the technician drives the car. These intermittent problems often reduce the fix to a guess. There are, however, devices similar to flight recorders which can be attached to the car's computer while it is being driven. When the problem occurs, the device registers and stores the data for analysis later by the technician. Unfortunately, not all problems fall within the scope of these devices.

Your car may not cooperate when you want it to exhibit a problem.

Training Credentials

Quality workmanship, as well as parts, are major considerations when choosing a repair shop. Are the people who work on your car qualified and well trained, or did they just do their first oil change this morning?

All car manufacturers sponsor training programs and technical clinics for their technicians on an ongoing basis. They may also have their own certification programs. Certified technicians have passed demanding written and hands-on tests in different categories.

The National Institute for Auto Service Excellence

(ASE) also certifies technicians through a series of eight written tests, each covering a different system of the car. Technicians must also have two years of hands-on work experience and be recertified every five years. Obviously, neither type of certification is a guarantee of competence, nor does it say anything about a technician's ethics. Still, certification is an indication of professionalism and certainly is better than nothing at all. Look for plaques on the shop's wall showing names and dates of certified technicians, or you may want to specifically ask to see a technician's credentials. Some of a shop's technicians may not be certified or may not be certified in all eight categories.

Rapport on Repairs

An equally important consideration in choosing a repair facility is attitude. Initial encounters should leave you feeling *comfortable* with the way you were treated. Were you listened to? Were you believed? Were you treated with respect and courtesy? Was the service writer or technician patient? Did she or he ask you pertinent questions that helped you to communicate about the problem that prompted your visit? If you and your service provider cannot establish a rapport on repairs, chances are the relationship won't last for long. A long-term association with a single repair shop or technician is the best way for them to get to know you and your car.

If you're still waiting for the fairy god-mechanic to appear, forget it. Start looking for the next best thing—a fair and good technician. You could turn your grim tales of automotive woe into stories that end with you happily driving off into the sunset.

Specialists Versus General Practitioners

Just as the medical world is full of specialists—doctors who only work on hearts, or ears, or feet—so, too, is the automotive world. The dealerships and independent

Just as the medical world has specialists and general practitioners, so too are there automotive shops which specialize in car makes or repair problems.

❖

repair shops that work only on a few makes of cars are most likely to have the trained technicians and updated technical information that it takes to work on today's computerized vehicles.

When it comes to certain items, such as tires, a specialist may be less expensive than an independent shop or dealership. High volume usually allows the specialty retailer to charge less and still make a profit. Call each and compare their prices. Always be sure that the prices you are comparing are for items of the same quality. If the specialty shop is using parts of inferior quality, those big savings in time and money may not be much of a bargain.

Guarantees

And finally, is the work guaranteed? Does the guarantee cover parts and labor? How long is the coverage in effect? A common practice is to guarantee work for 90 days. Is there anything you must do to keep the guarantee in force?

Keep in mind that there are two types of guarantees in the automotive business—the "property line guarantee"

Assemble as much information about your car as you can before you visit the repair shop. Be prepared.

❖

and an authentic guarantee. The property line guarantee is the one where, after the repairs have been completed, you get to the end of their property line, and they guarantee they never want to see you again! The authentic guarantee is the one that guarantees if the job is not done right the first time, the shop is accountable. They listen to you, believe you, and do their best to make the repair right.

Dealing with a Service Provider

Finding a good repair shop is essential, but it is not enough to ensure good car care. Make a maintenance log out of a spiral-bound notebook small enough to fit in the glove compartment or buy one in a store for a few dollars and change it to fit your needs. Record everything that happens to your car, for example, when you add fluids, oil, coolant, brake fluid, power steering fluid, and how much. Be specific. Just noting that oil was added isn't specific enough for you to track accurately. Record how much oil is added and its weight along with the date and the mileage (kilometers). Mark down which belts are changed, what filters are replaced, whether the front brakes or rear brakes are worked on, and any repairs that are made.

In the same notebook, keep track of your fuel economy. It's like keeping your finger on your car's pulse. A decrease in fuel economy over a short period of time is a sign that all is not well and will signal internal changes that may require simple adjustments or repairs to normalize them. If you record a drop of 10 percent in fuel economy over several fill-ups, bring it to the attention of your service provider.

You are in a far more powerful position to help the technician diagnose a problem if you've been keeping accurate records. Keeping records may seem like a pain in the neck at first, but after a while, it will be like brushing your teeth, a habit so ingrained that you would be uncomfortable not doing it.

Together with your manufacturer's service schedule, an up-to-date maintenance log is your best protection against unnecessary maintenance.

Warning! Do not assume that scheduled maintenance will automatically fix a problem. If you went to your doctor for your annual checkup and you had been having severe headaches for more than a month, would you expect the doctor to discover the problem without your communicating the symptoms? No, you'd need to carefully describe where the pain was, how often it occurred, and other specific circumstances that might shed some light on the problem. In the same way, when you bring your car in for scheduled service and there is a performance problem, be sure to tell your service provider about it. Supply as many pertinent details as you can. Doing this faithfully will go a long way toward keeping you out of the shop until the next scheduled service.

Use your five senses to detect as many symptoms as possible.

When used in conjunction with your manufacturer's schedule of service, an up-to-date maintenance log is also helpful in avoiding unnecessary maintenance and repairs. If someone tries to sell you a tire rotation in addition to the work you've requested, but you know your tires were rotated 2,000 miles (3,200 kilometers) ago and they're not due for rotation for another 5,500 miles (8,800 kilometers), you'll be able to say, "no thanks." Make a mental note to see if it happens again the future. Anyone can make a mistake, but a consistent pattern of attempts to oversell is a sure sign of greed and dishonesty.

Studies show that millions of dollars are lost every year because of misdiagnosed car problems. But you can keep this from happening to you. Just as technicians are not fairy godmothers, they are also not magicians or psychics or even private detectives. Before your technician can diagnose or fix the problem, he or she needs to know what symptoms have brought you and your car to the repair shop.

You can save time, money, and frustration by taking the time to clearly explain the symptoms or conditions that brought you to the service facility. Make sure the repair shop has all the information that you have. After all, who knows your car better than you do? You may not know what's wrong with it, but you do know when something is wrong with it.

Describing Symptoms

Using your five senses—hearing, sight, smell, taste, and touch—is the key to explaining your car's troubles to the technician and getting them solved.

Hearing: Noise is one of the more common ways your car will let you know it is not happy. Clicks, clunks, hisses, squeaks, squeals, rumbles, roars—yes, cars in pain do complain, but in their own language. Any of these sounds (or other unusual noises your car may create) could mean your car is heading for a breakdown or a repair. If the sound persists, you need to get the car inspected. Isolate the sound. Is it coming from the front,

Cars in pain do complain—often loudly.

rear, left, right, under the hood, inside the dash, in a wheel well, from the engine?

Touch: Does the car vibrate, shimmy, shake, sputter, surge, hesitate, stall, or continue running after you turn off the ignition? Is the car hard to steer or does the steering feel loose or sloppy? When you press the brake pedal, does it feel spongy or too hard? Does the pedal slowly sink to the floor after you've stopped?

Sight: Are your dashboard warning lights illuminated or flickering? Is the needle of any gauge out of its normal range? If so, you may have a problem with your battery, alternator, brakes, engine temperature, or oil pressure. Watch, too, for other signs of a problem, such as a leak. To identify where a leak is coming from, slide a piece of cardboard under the car and check it after a few hours. Note the source of the leak—front, rear, middle, left, right, a nearby garage shelf? Keep in mind that many leaks only occur under pressure at highway speeds.

What color is the leaking fluid? Brownish-black oil is either engine oil or steering fluid. A thick black ooze might be manual transmission fluid. A reddish, oily film is probably automatic transmission fluid. Coolant is generally green, pink, or yellow. Air conditioning discharge is clear.

Smell: If you have a leak, you might want to touch your finger to the spot on the ground and sniff the fluid. Most people can recognize the smell of gasoline. Coolant smells sweet. The smell of burning rubber may indicate

Is your dashboard trying to tell you something?

The vocabulary of your ailing car

overheated brakes or clutch. A sick catalytic converter often announces itself with the smell of rotten eggs.

Taste: If you have licked, nibbled, or eaten any part of your car for any reason, you probably need more help than a technician will be able to give you.

The Three Cs: Changes, Conditions, and Communications

Remember the three Cs when explaining your car's trouble symptoms.

Change: Change is often the first sign of a car problem. Does your car drink more fluids lately, such as gas, oil, coolant, transmission or brake fluid? Has your car suddenly become different in the way it handles or sounds? If it has always had a rattle in the rear end that sounds like your Uncle Harry trying to get out of the closet, you probably don't need to worry about it. But if you're driving down the road, and all of a sudden you hear a loud rattle, and it's getting worse by the minute, then you will probably want to have it checked. At least check the trunk. It could be a loose jack, or it really might be Uncle Harry.

Conditions: Under what conditions does the particular symptom occur? When you first start the car or after it has warmed up? When it's raining? When it's cold? Only when the heater is on? Only in first gear? Only on Tuesdays? When you're braking? Coasting? Accelerating?

Communications: After you've figured out as much as you can about what, how, when, and where your car's annoying symptom occurs, you must accurately communicate that information to your technician. Write everything down and give all the details. You might also want to tape a copy of the symptoms to the steering wheel. The person you talk to may not be the one who works on your car.

Remember the three Cs.

Here is an example of what you need to give your technician before anyone begins working on your car. Note these essential elements: (1) symptoms—as defined by the five senses and the three Cs above; (2) a telephone number where you can be reached; and (3) request for an estimate. The most technical term in the following letter is "tailpipe," proof that you don't need to study technical engineering to communicate satisfactorily to your technician.

Describe—Don't Diagnose

The second and last thing to remember about communications is: Describe—don't diagnose. If you had a stomachache, you wouldn't ask your doctor to remove your appendix, would you? No. You'd say you had a pain in your abdomen and that you were running a fever. The doctor would decide on the remedy.

The same is true of cars and technicians. If your car stalls and your neighbor tells you that when she had the exact same problem last month, the technician had to replace her car's fuel injectors, that doesn't mean you should walk into your service station and ask your technician to replace the fuel injectors. Your car might only

All right, all right, so we've taken a little poetic license on the fifth sense. Do not taste any automotive fluids or let any fluid touch an open sore or cut.

Dear Technician:

When I'm driving uphill at about 40 miles per hour (65 kilometers per hour), a whining sound comes from under the hood of my car which sounds like a big mosquito, then the car immediately stalls. It only does this on warm days (temperature above 50° F /10° C) and only after the car has been running for at least 15 minutes. After waiting at least a half hour, I am able to restart the car, at which time a big cloud of black smoke blows out of the tailpipe. Please call me at 555-1111 after your diagnosis to let me know how much you estimate the work will cost, if it will be more than $50. Thank you.

Sincerely,

Hope Itzminor

Garage-ese 101

Here are a few terms to help you describe your car's symptoms to a technician. (Turn to the glossary on page 226 to really improve your fluency in garage-ese.)

Engine Performance Terms

Afterfire—engine continues to fire after the vehicle has been turned off

Backfire—loud popping sound from the engine or tailpipe

Cuts out—irregular and complete loss of power

Dieseling—see *Afterfire*

Engine run on—see *Afterfire*

Fast idle—engine runs too fast

Hesitation—a pause or momentary lack of power

Miss—engine runs at speed erratically and unevenly

Power loss—engine continues to run but at dramatically reduced speed

Rough idle—slight engine vibration to severe shaking at a stop

Sluggish—power is less than normal, acceleration not as crisp as usual

Stall—engine dies completely

Stumble—engine starts to die and kicks back in before stalling

Surge—vehicle speeds up and slows down with no change in accelerator pedal pressure

Handling Terms

Bottoming—bottom of car scrapes the ground

Brake drag—brakes do not release completely

Brake fade—brakes take longer to stop the vehicle

Pitch—vehicle dives forward upon braking, or sideways upon cornering

Play—too much looseness in the steering wheel

Pull—vehicle strains to one side when braking

Shimmy—tires and steering wheel shake

Sway—vehicle continues to bounce after going over bump

Vibrate—vehicle shakes

Wander—vehicle drifts from side to side

Before you sign the repair order, go over it point by point and ask questions about any item you don't understand.

❖

need a minor adjustment or it may need something entirely different. *Tell the technician what your car is doing.* Describe the symptoms and let the technician make the diagnosis. The next time you have to visit the repair shop, make a checklist of your car's symptoms; see the sample checklist on the following page.

The troubleshooting charts included in this book are not intended to be exhaustive lists of problems or their causes. The charts are instead designed to familiarize you with some of the more common troublemakers. For many of the symptoms listed, there are 20 or 30 additional possible causes that are not included.

Don't Sign the Repair Order Yet

Talk things over before you act. Ask questions about the repair order before you sign it. Don't be afraid to say, "I don't understand what you mean by that."

Symptoms Checklist

Check as many symptoms as necessary.

1. WHAT IS VEHICLE DOING?   Description

☐ Noise _____

☐ Odor _____

☐ Visual _____

☐ Performance _____

☐ Handling _____

2. WHERE DOES IT COME FROM?

☐ Outside Car

    ☐ Engine compartment   ☐ Under the vehicle

    ☐ Left front   ☐ Left rear

    ☐ Right front   ☐ Right rear

    ☐ Center

☐ Inside Car

    ☐ Seat   ☐ Roof   ☐ Floor

    ☐ Door   ☐ Window   ☐ Windshield

    ☐ Instrument panel

3. WHEN DOES IT HAPPEN?

☐ When engine is being started   ☐ When engine is cold

☐ When engine is warming up   ☐ When engine is warmed up

☐ When engine is hot   ☐ Happens all the time

☐ After having driven for_____miles (kilometers)

☐ After having driven for___ minutes

☐ Changes with engine speed

☐ Changes with vehicle speed

☐ Only occurs when the vehicle is stopped

☐ Only occurs when accelerating

☐ Only occurs when decelerating

☐ When braking

☐ When cornering

☐ Intermittent—comes and goes with no obvious pattern

☐ At ____ mph (km/h)

☐ At any speed

☐ When using the clutch

☐ When in ____ gear

☐ When shifting from ___ gear into ___ gear

Read the repair order carefully before you sign it. Make certain it describes your car's trouble symptoms *specifically*. For example, the words "check engine performance" are too vague. They could mean anything. The repair order should *specifically* indicate the nature of the car's trouble symptoms—for example, "check for hesitation during first two minutes of engine warmup." It may also include the time of day, the speed, whether you're decelerating or accelerating, and how far you're traveled.

Ask for your old parts back (in a plastic bag for cleanliness, of course), but do so in advance. Remember that in asking to see the old part, you could actually be shown someone else's old part, but at least you'll be making it more awkward for a dishonest person to rip you off.

Get a written estimate. A repair order authorizes the service facility to perform the maintenance or repairs listed on it. When you sign a work order, you agree to be responsible for the charges listed on it. Ask questions about the work before you sign. And don't be afraid to take up some of their time. Service is their business.

NAME MARY NELSON			CUST. NO. 19252		R.O. DATE 7/23/98	MILEAGE 59125	TIME REC. 8:43	TIME PROM 2:00 PM
ADDRESS 5705 S. DELAWARE DRIVE			ADVISOR 1361	RESIDENCE PHONE 303·6654		BUSINESS PHONE 345·6843		
CITY, STATE SANTA FE , NM			ZIP 87501	V/E # 747564		DEL. MILEAGE 1		
YR 97	MAKE CHEV.	MODEL CAVA WGN	COLOR BRN	LICENSE *&/. BV	VEHICLE ID 1G1AD35P26727315			
LABOR RATE IS BASED ON AN AVERAGE OF $65.00 PER FLAT RATE HOUR ESTIMATE OF NEEDS REPAIRS								
QUANTITY	PART NO.		PRICE	EXTENSION		EMP. NO.	COST	
	Pickup Coil		$95.	/1978503				
	Modules		$160.	/1979107				
1.5	Labor		$97.50				97.50	
	Plug Wires		$60.					
	Plugs		$20.				65.00	
1.0	Labor		$65.					
	Air Filter		$18					
	EGR Valve		$66.					
.5	Labor		$32.50				32.50	
	TOTALS					TOTALS	614.00	

Get a written estimate.

Estimates, Guesstimates, and Second Opinions

If there are unknowns, get a written estimate. Many states have laws that require written estimates, at least for more expensive repairs. Other laws may also require shops to get your consent to exceed the estimate, return replaced parts, provide written invoices itemizing parts and labor, and more. Check with the attorney general's office for your state's requirements. You can't beat a written estimate for security.

Most shops will quote a flat-rate price for your work. Using a manual that averages the time it takes for each job, they will quote and charge you a set price rather than the clock rate or actual time it takes the mechanic to perform that procedure at a given hourly rate. If you have any questions about the flat-rate price, ask to see the manual. If the price differs from that in the manual, you have a right to know why. Just as the best waiter can make a mistake in a bill, so can the best service writer or mechanic. Why not double check as you would for any other bill?

"Take It Out and Tell You Later"

If a shop refuses and says they can't give you any kind of estimate until they pull the engine or transmission apart, consider taking your car elsewhere. (This strategy of "take it out and tell you later" may even be against the law in your state.) They may not be able to tell you what is wrong with the system until it is opened up; nevertheless, at a minimum, get an estimate in writing on the cost to disassemble, diagnose, and reassemble. Always find out what the maximum charge to you could be. Remember, you can always have the car towed to another shop. Never let yourself be intimidated or pressured into a repair job you feel uncertain about. Get a second opinion, even if it means the additional cost of a tow.

If the estimate is to be exceeded by a certain amount

or percentage (10 percent is a good rule of thumb), make sure you both agree that you must be notified and give your approval before the work is done. Leave a telephone number where you can be contacted and be there! Or agree on a time that you will call the mechanic to find out how things are going.

A Second Opinion

If you believe the estimate is high, are suspicious of the need for the repair, or simply want to compare prices, a second opinion makes sense. Yes, it's inconvenient and it's going to cost more money; however, the savings of hundreds of dollars or more may make it worthwhile if the original diagnosis was inaccurate or unreasonable.

It isn't always necessary to take the car to another shop, although you may want to, especially if the car is still driveable. Instead, you may be able to get a second opinion or compare a price over the telephone. First, talk to the shop and make sure you are quite clear about what the problem is, exactly what needs to be done to fix it, and how much it will cost. Write down all the information. Second, call another shop and ask what they charge to do the same repair. Be sure to give them the make, model, and year of your car first.

How to Pick Up Your Car after It Has Been Repaired

First, call the repair shop to make sure the car is ready. Allow yourself 20 minutes or more when you pick up your newly repaired car. You will need at least this much time to go over the bill and test drive the car. If you pick up your car one minute before the shop closes and then discover en route home that the problem you just paid for is still not fixed, you could find yourself talking to someone the next day who insists that the problem is a new one and intends to charge you accordingly. So arrive early whenever possible.

After you pick up your car from the shop, test drive it immediately.

The bill should be legible and understandable. A bill that is covered with smudged fingerprints and parts numbers without descriptions is not acceptable. Go over each item on the bill. If possible, speak to the person with you dealt with when you brought the car in for service. A good service provider should be willing to take the extra 10 or 15 minutes to explain, in plain English, the nature of the problem, what repairs were made, and how these steps related to your car's symptoms.

Listen to the explanations and if you don't understand them, be specific about exactly what it is you do not understand. There are no stupid questions. Ask to be shown (or drawn) a picture if words are failing. Keep asking until you are comfortable with your level of understanding. If you are satisfied with the work, let your service provider know it.

Test drive your car immediately. If you are not completely satisfied that the problem has been corrected, take your car back to the shop immediately.

If the Car Is Not Fixed Right the First, Second, or Even Third Time

Be assertive, not aggressive. Be firm, clear, and be specific about what is not right. Remember, you don't have to be disagreeable to disagree.

Request that the manager or shop foreman road test the vehicle with you in it to demonstrate that the problem has not been fixed correctly.

Give them a chance to correct the error or oversight; honest mistakes do happen. If the problem is not corrected to your satisfaction, you may need to take the following measures.

Keep Accurate Records

Keep accurate records, including all receipts and records. Include each service visit and an itemized list of what

LUBE, OIL AND FILTER CHANGES	DATE	MILEAGE/KILOMETERS	NOTES	OIL TYPE AND BRAND

AIR FILTER CHANGE	DATE	MILEAGE/KILOMETERS	NOTES

FUEL FILTER CHANGES	DATE	MILEAGE/KILOMETERS	NOTES

TIRE ROTATION	DATE	MILEAGE/KILOMETERS	NOTES

COOLING SYSTEM FLUSH AND REFILL	DATE	MILEAGE/KILOMETERS	NOTES

AUTOMATIC TRANSMISSION FLUID CHANGE AND FILTER	DATE	MILEAGE/KILOMETERS	NOTES

OTHER MAINTENANCE AND REPAIRS	DATE	MILEAGE/KILOMETERS	TYPE OF REPAIR OR MAINTENANCE	NOTES

Keep an up-to-date maintenance record and familiarize yourself with it before you have your car repaired.

There are many creative ways to voice dissatisfaction over repair service.

happened. Whenever possible, get a copy of the actual test results. Make certain the information includes any parts replaced and cost of labor, as well as what was said and who said it. Be sure you get the full name and title of the person with whom you speak. Date every piece of pertinent material, including each repair record. Do the same with every phone call.

Notify newspapers, radio and television consumer advocates, and private consumer groups of your problem. Be certain you send a copy of your letter to the repair shop.

Airing Your Complaints

Send the Better Business Bureau a copy of a letter stating the problem. Contact the Consumer Protection Agency (often a division of the attorney general's office). Ask them to refer you to any local complaint handling panels. Get as much information as possible about how the panel works, what kind of problems they handle, who handles them, how they are handled (whether by written or oral arguments), within what period of time they make their decisions, and whether they are binding on you and/or the other party.

If you are not satisfied with the results of the complaint panel, you may wish to take your claim to small claims court. You will not need a lawyer, but be certain your claim falls within the limits of the court.

If Your Car Is Under Warranty

Ask the dealership whether there are any technical service bulletins related to this problem. These TSBs are special information "communiqués" that describe fixes for unusual trouble areas. The manufacturer releases these to their dealerships. They can relate to anything from brakes to body work. If there are no TSBs issued for this particular problem, the technician should call the Technical Support Center for that manufacturer to advise. These folks specialize in the hard to fix areas and often have information that even the dealership does not. If a dealer tells you that your problem is a factory defect but there is no cure yet, be sure you get them to put it in writing.

Contact the manufacturer's customer service representative. The telephone number is usually found in your owner's manual. If you are still not satisfied, call or write the manufacturer's district or zone representative. (The name and telephone number may also be listed in your owner's manual. If not, ask the manufacturer's customer service representative for their number.) Document the details of the problem and ask the representative to meet with you to discuss them.

If you do not get a satisfactory response, pay for the cost of a written diagnosis from an independent mechanic. Do not, however, have the work done if the car is still under warranty.

Bringing in a Neutral Third Party

If you are still unsatisfied, take your case to the arbitration program of which your car manufacturer is a member. Arbitration programs are forums within which both the consumer and the dealer/manufacturer have an opportunity to state their side of the disagreement. These may be industry-run or state-run; the latter may require a filing fee. Depending on the car's warranty documentation, there may or may not be a choice as to which one to use. The jurisdiction of arbitration programs vary.

Check your warranty documents for details. If you must go to arbitration, get all the advice and information available by contacting the consumer affairs office of the state attorney general's office: how the procedure is conducted, who is on the panel, how the case is heard (whether by written or oral arguments), how long before a decision must be rendered, and if you must accept the findings of the panel. Usually decisions are binding for the manufacturer, but not for the consumer. The most important part of these proceedings is that you follow

Most states have passed lemon laws.

the rules of the arbitration board to the letter and that your case is well documented.

Lemon Laws

To protect consumers from manufacturer's defects in new vehicles, most states have passed lemon laws. These laws cover problems that are so serious they result in the loss or reduction of the vehicle's use, value, and/or safety. Further, they prescribe methods for compensation of the cost of repairs and related expenses, and in some cases, they even recommend the replacement of the vehicle or the refund of its value.

The specific requirements for asserting your rights under the lemon laws vary from state to state. The cover-

Arbitration and Dispute Resolution Offices

Chrysler Customer Arbitration Board
Consult owner information packet or call Chrysler Customer Center:
(800) 992-1997

Ford Dispute Settlement Board
P.O. Box 5120
Southfield, MI 48086
(800) 241-8450

Better Business Bureau Auto Line
(800) 955-5100
Participating manufacturers (national): Acura, Alfa-Romeo, Audi, General Motors, Honda, Infiniti, Isuzu, Nissan, Saturn, Volkswagen. (BMW, Jaguar, Maserati, Mitsubishi, Peugeot, Land Rover, Rolls-Royce, Saab, Sterling, Subaru, and Volvo also participate in certain states.)

National Automotive Dealers Association
8400 Westpark Drive
McLean, VA 22102
(800) 254-NADA
Participating manufacturers:
Acura, BMW, Fiat, Honda, Isuzu, Jaguar, Mitsubishi, Nissan, Rolls-Royce, Saab, Volvo.

age time may be as brief as one year or as long as two years from the date of ownership or warranty period. An authorized facility must have unsuccessfully attempted to make repairs for the same or different problem (this depends on how the state law is written) a predetermined number of times, or the car must be out of service and in the shop for a specific number of days during the coverage time. The dealer or manufacturer must be correctly notified of the problem and given the opportunity to fix it. This may mean a certified return receipt letter to the dealer, the manufacturer's customer relations office, and the local district or zone representative. Arbitration is the standard forum for resolution. If you believe your vehicle qualifies under your state's lemon law, contact your state attorney general's office and get all information related to filing a complaint. However, it is not necessary for your state to have a lemon law for you to participate in arbitration.

If your problem is safety related, call the National Highway Safety Administration's toll-free number, (800) 424-9393. They can give you information about safety standards, regulations, recalls, and references to other governmental agencies that can assist you in problem solving.

Tips on Avoiding Car Repair Rip-off

➤ Ask neighbors, friends, and family members to recommend reputable repair shops.

➤ Check out the repair shop before you leave your car there. How long has the company been in business? Ask about training, certification, warranties offered, and the kind of equipment they use.

➤ Keep a maintenance log of all service work done on your car.

➤ Get a written estimate and read the repair order. Make sure you understand all of it.

➤ Don't expect perfection. Even the best technicians sometimes make mistakes.

➤ If you are dissatisfied with your service and can't get satisfaction, write a letter to the company manager or president.

➤ Consider legal action as a last resort. Many repair shops will agree to resolve disputes through mediation or arbitration.

16
SAFETY ON AND OFF THE ROAD

It's currently hip to sit high off the road in an SUV. It's presently smart to run with chromed wheels. And in some circles it's considered snazzy if your personalized license plates are clever—for this season anyway.

But being safe and feeling secure are here to stay—and unaffected by fashion. Car safety has come a long way in recent years. Redesigned and reinforced vehicle structures, the widespread use of seat belts, active head restraints, dual front air bags, side air bags, antilock brakes, and traction control are just a few of the many important technical advances that are keeping us safer. If you drive alone, you can improve your personal safety by taking a few simple precautions.

Sometimes, today's highways can feel like a war zone.

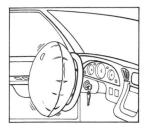

When even uttering the words air bag, think in the same breath seat belts. Air bags are not as effective if seat belts are not properly fastened.

While some active and passive safety features, such as air bags and antilock brakes, have recently received much negative press, these features by and large are highly effective in doing what they were designed to do—prevent serious injury or death or prevent an accident in the first place. Some safety systems are largely misunderstood—often due to the lack of proper training of car salespeople and drivers. But armed with good information, common sense, and preparation, you can meet the challenges of today's fast-paced highways.

Safety has come a long way in recent years. Redesigned vehicle structures, the widespread use of seat belts, air bags, antilock brakes, and traction control are helping vehicles to grip even slippery roads. Collapsible steering columns and shatterproof safety glass have all contributed to protecting occupants during accidents. But protection is only part of the effort. Breakthroughs in crash avoidance technology are also taking place. Sophisticated radar can detect obstacles that are too close for comfort—or rather for safety. Onboard navigation systems, such as GM's Onstar™, that tell us where we are and how to get where we want to go are already in use on some vehicles.

Despite advances, however, driving remains one of the more dangerous activities we engage in. Our stress levels

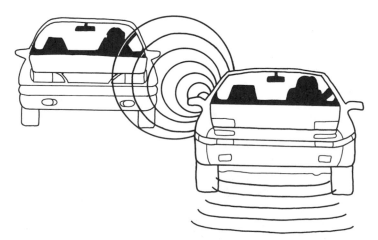

In parking-assist systems, microwaves detect obstacles that are too close for comfort, enhancing a driver's senses.

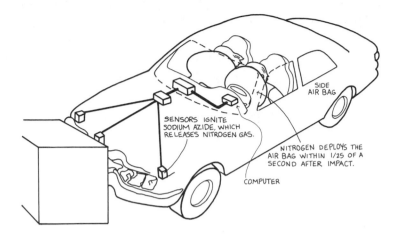

SIDE
AIR BAG

SENSORS IGNITE
SODIUM AZIDE, WHICH
RELEASES NITROGEN GAS.

NITROGEN DEPLOYS THE
AIR BAG WITHIN 1/25 OF A
SECOND AFTER IMPACT.

COMPUTER

How air bags work
❖

have risen due to overcrowded highways. And at night, the stress is compounded by our awareness that our personal safety if often at risk. That risk has been heightened as the level and frequency of auto-related violence has increased.

Keeping your car well maintained, your gas tank at least a quarter full, and your tires properly inflated are essential ingredients of being prepared. *Note:* Being suspicious of coincidence and aware of your surroundings are just as important. But even if you conscientiously follow these general guidelines, you may have to deal with an emergency situation.

If you drive alone, you can improve personal safety by taking a few simple precautions:

➤ Consider purchasing membership in an auto club or 24-hour towing assistance program. On most newer cars, these assistance programs are free for a limited period of time.

➤ Never leave your car running.

➤ Never leave your keys in the car.

➤ Never leave your car unlocked.

Caution!

A rear-facing child car seat should never be placed in the front passenger seat of any vehicle equipped with a standard passenger-side front air bag. Nor should children under 13 ride in the front seat.

For more information on child safety seats:
Child Safety Seats
National Highway
Traffic and Safety
Administration
400 Seventh St. SW
Washington, DC 20590
800/424-9393

Glossary of Safety Features

antilock brake system (ABS): electronically controlled brakes that prevent wheels from locking up and vehicles from skidding during emergency braking. When used correctly, antilock brakes may be the most important safety feature developed in modern times, next to seat belts.

daytime running lights: high-beam headlights that operate when your car is in motion—but with reduced output. Mandatory in many countries, these lights reduce the chance of a crash by increasing your visibility.

de-powered air bags: air bags that have had some force removed to reduce air bag–related injuries and deaths of small adults and young children

electronic keys: The ultimate in security and theft protection, keys that allow a vehicle to start only with a perfect match between a transponder embedded in the ignition key and the vehicle's ignition.

integrated remote controls: systems that increase security and safety by opening garage doors and turning on selected interior home lamps

navigational computers: satellite-operated systems that can guide you to the nearest hotel or Italian restaurant, tell you how to avoid traffic jams, unlock vehicles that have been inadvertently locked, track a stolen vehicle, direct you through a strange city, and automatically send help if you are in an accident

parking assist: a system that uses microwaves to measure distances between your car and nearby objects (such as another vehicle, a bicycle, or a child in the driveway). Audible and visual indicators warn you as you reverse or nudge forward in tight spots.

Navigational computers can be your "third eye" on the road.

rain-sensing wipers: wipers that automatically adjust from high speed to a no-wipe position via an infrared beam that calculates the amount of moisture on the windshield

self-dimming rearview mirrors: mirrors that work on the same principle as photo-gray sunglasses. The glass surface dims when hit by the bright light of a vehicle from behind and returns to normal when the light disappears.

side air bags: initiated by crashes from all directions other than full rear, air bags that protect occupants by popping out of the door or the back of the front seat.

smart air bags: also called "bags with a brain," devices that can differentiate between the weight of an adult or child, a rear-facing child car seat, and an empty passenger seat. Controlled by sensors, they deploy only if the weight calls for action.

stability control: a computer-controlled system responsible for keeping a vehicle on course. The system works in conjunction with antilock brakes. Electronic sensors monitor the speed and direction of the wheels, as well as the vehicle's yaw (sideways motion in a curve). When the system senses a deviation from the driver's intended course, it instantly slows an individual wheel or reduces engine power, thereby returning the vehicle to the desired direction.

xenon headlamps: low-beam headlamps that approximate natural daylight. With their blue-white light, xenon headlamps are considered the best and the brightest.

Some computer-controlled suspensions actively help keep vehicles on the driver's intended course.

Note!

There is only one rule that always applies: your safety and that of your passengers comes first.

➤ Always lock yourself in the car. (Power door locks are an excellent safety feature.)

➤ When you drive into a parking lot, notice the other cars, especially if they are occupied.

➤ Always park in a well-lighted central spot, preferably one where there are frequent passersby.

➤ When returning to your car, keep your keys in your hand with the sharp ends protruding between your fingers. They make a good weapon.

➤ As you drive away, notice the behavior of other cars.

➤ If you suspect you are being followed, go to a public place and request that the manager call the police.

➤ When stopped at a stoplight, leave enough room between you and the car in front of you to be able to maneuver around it if trouble does develop.

➤ Never pick up hitchhikers. If you must for any reason talk to a stranger while you are in your vehicle, lower the window only the inch or so required to be heard.

➤ If you see someone in distress on the highway, drive to the nearest police or service station and report their plight to someone who can help them, or notify authorities on your cell phone.

If your vehicle is hit from behind by another car at a stoplight or sign, do not get out of the car.

If you suspect you are being followed, go to a public place and request that the manager call the police.

❖

➤ If your vehicle is hit from behind, roll the window down only enough to be heard, and request the driver to follow you to the nearest police station or public place.

➤ As you drive, get in the habit of making mental notes of route numbers, locations of service stations, emergency telephones, and police stations.

➤ If you are harassed in any way, do not respond. Appear to be uninterested—not disdainful. Most of these people are looking for a reaction. If they continue to harass you, drive to a public place and have someone telephone the police.

➤ Avoid shortcuts that take you through unfamiliar or unsafe areas.

➤ If you have a garage, consider having an automatic garage door opener installed. When using an automatic garage door opener, remain in the car until the garage door has closed behind you.

➤ Consider investing your time and money in one of the top driving schools. Check the automobile magazines for names and addresses.

If you drive alone, you can increase your safety by taking a few simple precautions, such as parking under a streetlight at night.

➤ Buy a cell phone and use it only for emergencies—
yours and others!

Road Rage

Contrary to current belief, bad manners, ill tempers, and
stupid moves have been with us ever since the advent of
the Model T. "Road rage" is not new—just the term is.
However, it may be getting scarier out there. Recent polls
suggest that up to 74 percent of Americans think that drivers are getting more aggressive.

But just as you read this and decide to ride the bus,
read on. It is also true that better cars, better highways,
and stricter drunk-driving laws are working in our favor.

Your own attitude can also make a difference. The
next time someone takes "your" parking space or tail-
gates, drive around the block and look for another space,
pull over and let the "bumper hugger" go by, and give

**Your emergency kit should include a first aid kit, flares or
a reflective triangle, plastic chock, a flashlight and spare
batteries, jumper cables, a distress flag or cloth, and a
sign or auto shade that reads "Help, Call Police."**

the other driver a break. Drive consciously and conscientiously, not competitively.

Dealing with the Dreaded Flat Tire

You're driving down the road, it's late at night, and you hear a loud *pop*. The car swerves violently. You take your foot off the accelerator and with firm, steady, but relaxed arms, you pick a safe spot on the side of the road and ease the car over to it.

Right now a cellular phone and the 800 number for a 24-hour towing service would look like the best investment you'd ever made, but failing that, here is what you can do to get back on the road. Immediately after stopping, put the emergency flashers on and set the parking brake with the car turned off and in park or first gear. After exiting the car by the door away from the road, you pull out your fully equipped emergency kit. In it is a good flashlight with batteries that work! You take the piece of fluorescent material—vest, ribbon, anything you can drape over your body—and put it on so you show up in the dark. (Flat tires only happen when you're in your best dark-colored outfit.) Now take one of the two flares from the emergency kit, or the plastic reflective triangle.

You walk backward six to ten car lengths and position the triangle or flare so that it can be easily seen by oncoming traffic. If you are using flares, light the first of the two flares as you would a big match. First take the top plastic cover off. You'll find a striking surface underneath. Now remove the second, larger, plastic cover under which you will find another striking surface. Hold the flare away from your face and briskly rub striking surface against striking surface. The flare may spit sparks at you, so keep it away from your clothing as you stick it in the ground or lay it on its side. Most flares will burn for only 15 minutes. That's why you have two.

Remove the instructions for the use of your jack from the glove box or wherever they are located. It will

Some of the worst hazards on the road are angry drivers.

In the event of a flat tire, pull off the road with your emergency flashers on.

❖

help if you have practiced the following procedure in the warmth and comfort of your own well-lighted driveway or garage with several of your closest friends for company. It will also help if you purchased a four-way (star) lug wrench that day last spring at a local auto parts or retail store. You will have had two choices when you bought yours: one is for domestic vehicles (SAE) and one is for imported vehicles (metric). What? You don't have one? Get thee to a parts store. Tell the service personnel the make of your vehicle you are driving, and they will guide you to the best choice.

Ready? Good. Here's what you do:

1. Remove all the required paraphernalia: jack, lug wrench, spare tire, chock (block), and garden gloves (optional).
2. Place the chock behind the wheel that is diagonally opposite (kitty-corner to) the one that is flat. This is to ensure that even if the car does slip off the jack, it won't roll.
3. Remove the wheel covering using the method and device shown in your manual; keep it handy. If your vehicle has aluminum wheels, you will need to use the special aluminum wheel lock located in a plastic bag in the glove box, owner's manual pouch, or with the spare tire.

With practice, you can change a flat tire in about 10 minutes. Helpful hint: practice in your driveway, not on a moonlit freeway.

4. Position the jack as your manual indicates, but do not raise the car with it yet.

5. First, break the tension on the lug nuts, *but don't remove them.* Since they have undoubtedly been put on with an air tool, which has the strength of eight giant weightlifters, you will need to use a length of pipe or the special star wrench to increase your leverage. The end of the wrench should fit snugly onto the lug nuts. Remember, "right is tight." Loosen the lug nuts by turning them to the left, or counter-clockwise. The only exception, and this is rare, is if the lug nuts are labeled with an "L." If they are, you will need to loosen them in the opposite direction.

Changing a tire, in ten easy steps (steps 1-5)

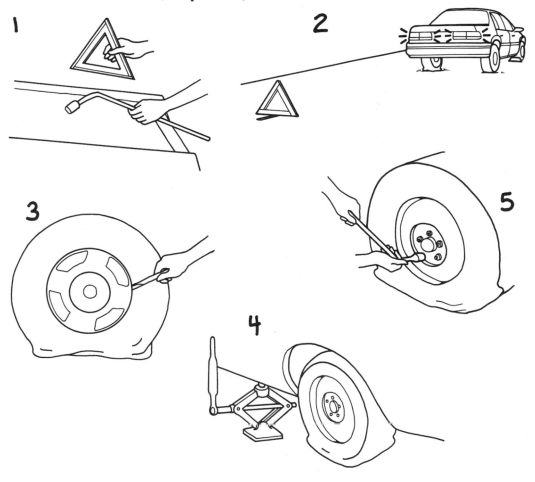

Changing a tire
(steps 6-10)

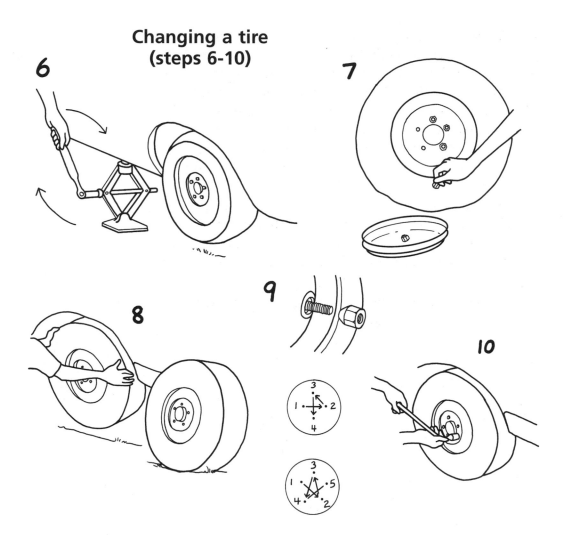

6. Now, *slowly* engage the jack, standing slightly to one side in case the jack decides to let go. Raise the car only as high as necessary to remove the old tire and to put the new one on. You can always raise it another notch if it's too low to the ground, but the higher it goes, the less stable it is.

7. Remove the lug nuts the rest of the way by hand and put them inside the hub cap. If you miss this step and you accidentally kick one into the dirt, you can bet trying to find it in the dark will be less than amusing.

8. Take the damaged tire off. Be particularly careful not to touch the rubber until you're sure it's cool.

Blowouts increase tire temperatures to tropical levels, and they may remain hot for quite a while. This is why we recommend having a pair of garden gloves.

9. Put the spare on. Hand-tighten the lug nuts in a *criss-cross* pattern until each one starts to make the wheel spin. Then go back and check each one again.

10. Slowly lower the jack. Take the lug wrench and tighten each one of the lugs with as much force as you can muster. As long as the lug wrench is at a right angle to the wheel, you shouldn't do any damage. Right is tight (with the above-mentioned exception).

As soon as you stow the equipment back where it came from, you can be on your way. Drive to a service station and have the original tire repaired. If the spare is a full-sized spare that can be rotated into your regular tires, you can continue to drive on it, but have the tension on the lug nuts checked by a professional as soon as possible.

If there is no safe place to pull off the road—let's say you're stuck on a narrow bridge—you will have to continue to drive the car at a reduced speed with the emergency flashers on until you reach a safe spot to pull off the road. That means the tire will probably get damaged and possibly the wheel as well—but a ruined tire is a small price to pay for your safety.

If, for whatever reason, you do not feel comfortable with the above procedure or if your vehicle has quit for a reason other than a flat tire, consider using Plan B.

Plan B: Use your emergency flashers to alert other drivers that your vehicle is disabled. Take the fluorescent sign that is also in your emergency kit—the one that says "Help, Please Call Police"—and place it in the rear window so that the traffic going in your direction can easily see it. Lock your door, and open it only for a uniformed policeman or legitimate tow truck representative. If someone else stops to help you, the safest thing you can do under most circumstances is to remain in the car and speak with them only through an inch or so of rolled-down window (enough for you to be heard). Thank them for their offer of help and ask them to call the police and tow truck.

Warning!

Do not attempt to jump-start or recharge a battery when the indicator is clear. It generally means the battery is low on water, and high on hydrogen gas. A spark could cause an explosion.

Jump-starting a Battery

Keeping up with routine maintenance will hopefully keep you from ever having to jump-start your car, but you should know the procedure in case an emergency presents itself.

Move the two cars close, *but do not allow them to touch.* Turn off the ignition and all electrical accessories except for the emergency flashers if needed.

All batteries and jumper cables are color coded. Red is positive. Black is negative. Here's how to jump-start a battery:

1. Connect the red jumper cable first to the dead battery's positive terminal.

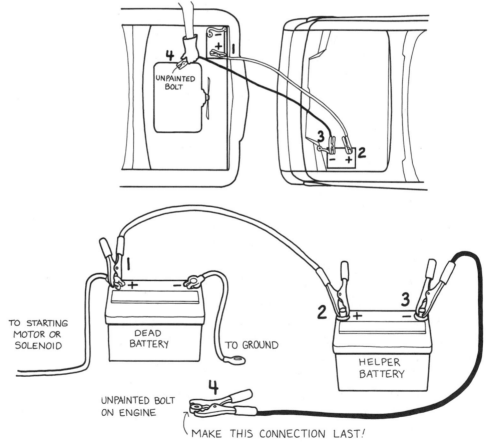

How to jump-start a battery

2. Connect the other end of the red jumper cable to the positive terminal of the helper battery.
3. Connect the black jumper cable to the negative terminal of the helper battery.
4. Connect the other end of the black jumper cable to an unpainted piece of metal (a bolt is a good choice) on the stalled engine.
5. Start the helper car, then the stalled car.
6. Remove jumper cables in the exact *opposite order.*

Electrical Fire

If you notice a fire under the hood—and, if one were burning, chances are you would—drive the car to a safe area, stop, pull the inside hood latch, and get yourself and your passengers out of the car and to safety immediately. Go to the nearest phone and call the fire department. Do *not* open the hood of the car. The extra oxygen that is added by opening the hood may feed the fire. You have already helped by releasing the hood's interior latch. Stay away from the car while you wait the arrival of the fire department and let professionals put the fire out.

GLOSSARY

afterfire: the tendency of an engine to continue running after the key has been turned off; also called dieseling or engine run-on

aftermarket: describes an automotive part or accessory built by someone other than a new-car manufacturer

air-conditioning condenser: a device that condenses refrigerant gas, causing it to give up heat as it turns to liquid

air filter: pleated folds of paper designed to catch dust and dirt before they enter an engine

alignment: *see* wheel alignment

alternator: a motor that produces electric current for storage by the battery

amperes (amps): a measurement of electrical current or flow

antenna: an externally mounted rod or a wire embedded in glass, used to receive radio signals

antifreeze: a substance, usually ethylene glycol, added to a car's water cooling system to keep it from freezing in winter and boiling over in summer

antilock brake system (ABS): electronically controlled brakes that help drivers maintain steering control and prevent wheel lock-up during hard braking

arc: the discharge of an electric current across an air gap

audible theft deterrent system: an alarm system that sounds the horn or a siren at frequent intervals while the headlights flash in tandem

auto-down/up windows: a feature that lets users fully open or close windows with a single touch

automatic electrochromic dimming mirror: a mirror that responds to different amounts of light, darkening to reduce nighttime headlight glare

automatic exterior lighting: a dash-mounted photoelectric cell system that turns headlights off and on when lighting conditions change. The system can also come with an adjustable-delay security feature that keeps lights on for a given time.

automatic transmission: a transmission in which gears are shifted automatically by the engine's torque converter

auxiliary 12-volt power outlet: an outlet that allows drivers to use a portable telephone, computer, or fax machine

axle: the rod or shaft on which a wheel is mounted

backfire: an explosion of the air/fuel mixture heard at the tailpipe or under the hood

balance shaft: a shaft that uses weights to spread out the vibrations produced by an engine

ball joints: a coupling or pivoting device that permits movement between suspension components

battery: a device that stores electricity generated by the alternator and releases it to the car's electrical system

battery run-down protection: a system that turns off an electrical drain on a vehicle, thereby saving the battery charge

bead: the metal-reinforced inner rim of a tire that holds it on the wheel and provides an airtight seal

bearing: a machine part that supports another part while allowing it to rotate, as a wheel on an axle or a piston on a crankshaft

bias-belted tire: a tire whose plies meet each other on the diagonal, reinforced with strips of metal or fiberglass

bonding: a gluing process

boot: a rubber sleeve that covers and protects front-end parts like CV joints, tie rod ends, and ball joints

brake fade: loss of brake effectiveness as a result of heavy use

brake lights: red lights located at the rear of a vehicle

brake horsepower (BHP): the amount of power an engine delivers after taking into account the forces of friction, including inertia and wind resistance that warn following vehicles that the driver is braking

brake lines: noncorrosive stainless steel tubing that carries brake fluid from the master cylinder to the brakes at each wheel

brake lining: heat-resistant material that lines the moving parts (shoes) of drum brakes

brake shoe: a crescent-shaped piece of metal lined with heat-resistant materials

break in: the period in a new vehicle's life during which the engine's friction-bearing surfaces settle into place. Unusual stress during break in can shorten engine life.

bumper: a metal bar at the front or rear of a vehicle that helps limit damage in a minor collision. The bumper is usually camouflaged with sturdy body-color plastic or rubber.

bumper-to-bumper warranty: the manufacturer's guarantee that everything in a vehicle, from the front bumper to the rear bumper (except for "normal wear and tear" items and those that are specifically excluded), will be free of defects and perform in a specific way

bushing: a metal doughnut or rubber liner that reduces wear between two metal parts by acting as a cushion

caliper: a brake component that works like a fist, with one or two fingers (pistons) that force disc brake pads against the rotor, causing it to slow or stop the vehicle

camshaft: a rotating bar or shaft with bumps or lobes (called cams) that regulate the opening and closing of the engine's valves. Engines are often classified by the number and position of the camshafts within the engine.

capacitor: *see* condenser

carbon deposits: the natural accumulation of the byproducts of combustion within the engine. Over time these deposits can adversely affect engine performance.

carburetor: a device that combines air and fuel and distributes this mixture to the cylinders. Carburetors are usually found in older model vehicles, as they have now been replaced by fuel injectors.

catalytic converter: a pollution control device located along the exhaust pipe. It contains exotic metals and chemically treated substances that turn pollutants into such harmless substances as water and carbon dioxide.

cell: a device that produces electric current. Most batteries have six cells that are connected. Also a unit of memory in a computer.

CFC-free: refers to an environmentally friendly refrigerant (replacing Freon) used in modern air-conditioning systems

chassis: the steel frame or platform of an automobile. Full-frame chassis are still found on most trucks but have been replaced in most passenger vehicles by unibody construction.

child safety door lock: a switch on a rear doorjamb that allows the door or window to be opened only from the outside

choke: a heat-sensitive door or plate on top of the carburetor that closes when it is cold, forcing more gasoline into the air/fuel mixture

circuit: the path of an electrical current from its source, through various electronic devices, and finally back to its source

clear-coat paint: clear protective paint over the body color

clutch: in manual transmissions, a device that disengages the engine from the driveshaft while the driver shifts gears

clutch plate: a disc covered with friction-producing material that is squeezed against the flywheel when the clutch pedal is released. This action connects the engine and the transmission.

coil: a booster or magnifier of electrical current that supplies high-voltage electricity to the spark plugs

coil spring: a suspension component that compresses and extends in response to irregularities in the road surface

combustion: the burning of the air/fuel mixture

combustion chamber: the upper area within the cylinders where the air/fuel mixture is burned

composite body panels: rust-free, lightweight, flexible composite materials that protect against minor dings and dents

composite headlights: small unconventional bulbs that allow designers to shape the glass area of a headlight in limitless ways

compression: the squeezing or compressing of the air/fuel mixture by the pistons to facilitate combustion

compression ratio: the volume of a cylinder when the piston is at its lowest point of travel compared with the volume of the cylinder when the piston is at its highest point of travel; expressed in a ratio such as 12:1. In general, the higher the number, the more powerful the engine.

compression stroke: the upward movement of a piston that compresses the fuel mixture into a small space at the top of the combustion chamber

compressor: a machine that compresses gas; found in vehicle air conditioning systems

condenser: an electrical device that acts like a tiny sponge, receiving and storing electricity

conductor: any material that offers little resistance to the flow of electricity

connecting rod: a metal piece that connects the piston to the crankshaft

conventional spare tire: a wheel and tire exactly the same size as those "on the ground" (as opposed to space-saving, compact, limited-mileage spares)

cornering lamp: a lamp mounted up front on some models that throws out a wide beam of white light sideways to indicate a lane change or illuminate the entrance to a darkened driveway

constant velocity joint (CV joint): the flexible joint on the driveshaft of a front-wheel-drive vehicle that allows the wheels to turn and move up and down

control arms: metal arms that attach the wheels to the frame of a car

coolant: a solution of water and ethylene glycol that draws heat away from the engine

coolant reservoir: a translucent container that serves as an overflow reservoir for expanding coolant

cooling system: components that help keep an engine from overheating. The major elements are the radiator, radiator cap, thermostat, and water pump.

coupe: a two-door sedan whose front seats fold forward for access to the back seat

crankcase: the metal casing surrounding the crankshaft

crankshaft: the bar to which the pistons are attached. The crankshaft converts the up-and-down motion of the pistons into rotational motion.

crankshaft balancer: a weighted object attached to a crankshaft to smooth out the vibrations of the engine; also called a harmonic balancer

crumple zones: areas at the front and rear of a vehicle that are designed to fold up to absorb and redirect crash forces

curb weight: the weight of the standard-equipped vehicle with a full tank of fuel and no passengers

current: the flow of electricity in a circuit

cutting: shaving off a thin layer of metal from the brake rotors or drums to remove surface irregularities; also known as turning or machining

cylinder: a hollow tube cut into the engine block that contains the piston

cylinder block: the lower portion of the engine containing the pistons, crankshaft, and other engine parts, as well as the lubrication and cooling passages

cylinder head: the top portion of the engine in which the valves and, in many engines, the camshafts are located. Many modern cylinder heads contain aluminum components.

daytime running lights: headlights that automatically turn on at less than full power to increase visibility

delayed accessory power: a system that allows operation of certain accessories for up to 10 minutes after turning off ignition or until a door is opened

detonation: severe engine knock or pinging caused by irregular burning of the air/fuel mixture

depowered front air bags: air bags with reduced power to help protect properly belted small adults and children from injury

diesel engine: an engine in which the air/fuel mixture is ignited without spark plugs, by raising its temperature and pressure within the combustion chamber. Although not readily available, diesel engines are premium-priced alternatives that give better mileage and run "cooler" and cleaner

differential: a specialized set of gears that pass power from the engine to the wheels. The device allows a car's outside wheels to travel farther and faster than the inside wheels while cornering.

dimmer switch: a switch or control arm that changes headlights from low to high beam and back again

dipstick: a rod used for measuring the volume of a vehicle's fluids

disc brake: a brake consisting of a disc (the rotor) attached to a wheel, which is squeezed by a caliper to slow or stop the car. Disc brakes are usually found on front wheels but are increasingly found on front and rear wheels.

distributor: the ignition component that distributes voltage to the spark plugs

distributor cap: the plastic cap covering the distributor, to which the spark plug wires are attached. In newer vehicles the engine computer has taken over its task.

distributorless ignition: a modern ignition system in which a computer performs the tasks of the distributor

drag: usually called the coefficient of drag, this is a measurement of a vehicle's air or wind resistance. The smaller the number the more aerodynamic the vehicle.

driveability: refers to a variety of performance problems that cannot be readily diagnosed or easily fixed

drive belt: also called a V-belt, a belt that transfers power from the engine to an accessory such as the fan, water pump, or power steering pump. On newer vehicles these are also called serpentine belts.

driveshaft: the bar that connects the transmission to the differential in a rear-wheel-drive vehicle

driving lamps: also called fog lamps, auxiliary front lamps for high speed night driving

drum brakes: a type of brake that uses a drum-shaped canister mounted on the wheel and two crescent-shaped brake shoes to stop a vehicle

dry gas: an alcohol additive that helps prevent gas line freeze-up by absorbing water in the fuel supply

dual overhead cam engine (DOHC): a common layout for multivalve engines in which the two camshafts that open and close the valves are located above the valves

dual-zone climate control: an air-conditioning/heating system that allows a front-seat passenger a choice of temperature

dynamometer (dyno): a diagnostic machine that measures the torque and horse-power of a vehicle

electrolyte: in the battery, a solution of water and sulfuric acid that causes the opposite charges of the different plate metals to react chemically

electronic ignition: a system for delivering voltage to the spark plugs more reliably and precisely; controlled by sophisticated computers

emission controls: devices that reduce pollutants or chemically change them into less harmful substances

engine analyzer: a device used to diagnose engine performance problems

engine block: the lower part of the engine, where the pistons and cylinders are located

engine block heater: a device that keeps the engine block warm to ensure quick starts on frigid winter mornings, instant cabin warmth, and quick effective defrost

engine control module (ECM): the heart of the engine's main computer, this component interprets engine data from sensors and regulates the air/fuel mixture, ignition timing, and other systems; also called an engine control unit (ECU). A failure will turn on the Check Engine or Service Engine Soon light.

engine head: a heavy metal casting bolted to the engine block that covers the cylinders and forms the top of the combustion chamber. The valves and spark plugs are attached to the engine head.

ergonomics: the study of the interaction and the ease of operation between machines and humans

ethanol: a specially formulated gasoline additive containing grain alcohol that helps reduce pollutants

evaporative emission control system: a system that traps fuel vapors from the gas tank when the engine isn't running and releases them to be burned after the engine starts

exhaust gas emissions analyzer: an emissions testing device that can be used to determine internal engine damage by detecting the presence of exhaust gases in the radiator

exhaust gas recirculation (EGR) system: a system that redirects partially burned exhaust gases back to the engine, where they are burned again

exhaust manifold: a set of metal pipes that route exhaust gases away from the engine on their way to the catalytic converter and muffler

exhaust system: a series of components that route burned gases away from the engine

exhaust valve: a valve (or one-way door) through which burned gases exit the combustion chamber

expansion valve: the valve (or one-way door) in an air-conditioning system that regulates the flow of refrigerant into the evaporator

evaporator: an air-conditioning component that turns refrigerant from a liquid into a gas to remove heat from the passenger compartment

fail-safe cooling system: a feature that allows a "limp home" time frame without damage to an engine that has lost coolant

feedback carburetor: a carburetor assisted by an external computer

firing order: the sequence in which the spark plugs fire

fittings: places where metal parts are joined together

flashing unit: a switch that controls the directional signal light bulbs, turning them on and off from 60 to 120 times a minute

flywheel: a large, heavy disk that is attached to the crankshaft and presses against the clutch plate

four-wheel drive: a power train that transfers power to all four wheels

friction: the rubbing of one object against another, generating heat and resulting in wear

front end: the steering and suspension components of a vehicle

front-wheel drive: a power train that transfers power to a car's front wheels

fuel filler cap: the removable screw cap that allows you to fill your fuel tank; an integral part of a vehicle's evaporative emission system

fuel filter: the filter that cleans gasoline by catching dirt and foreign particles before they reach the working parts of the carburetor or fuel injectors

fuel injection: a method of supplying fuel to an engine by injecting it into the intake manifold just above the cylinders. This system is the modern equivalent of a carburetor.

fuel injector: a device that squirts fuel into the engine in a fuel injection system

fuel lines: lines that carry fuel from the fuel tank to the engine

fuel pump: the mechanism that draws fuel from the fuel tank to the engine. It may be mechanically or electrically powered.

fuel sock: a coarse filter located in the fuel tank

fuse: a thin wire encased in plastic or glass that protects the electrical system from excess electricity

fuse box: a container within the vehicle's cabin that holds fuses and often spares

fusible link: a light piece of wire placed in a circuit that melts in response to surges of electricity; similar to a fuse but without a protective casing

gasket: a thin flat piece of material that acts as a seal between two joined surfaces

gas line freeze-up: the formation of ice crystals in gasoline during cold weather. The condition starves the engine of fuel by clogging fuel lines.

gas-powered shock absorber: a highly efficient shock absorber that uses a nitrogen charge to pressurize the fluid in the tubes

gear ratio: the number of turns a driving gear makes compared to the number made by the driven gear

gears: metal-toothed wheels used to transmit turning power

glazing: a hard, icelike substance that forms on belts, clutch discs, and brake pads and resists melting. Glazing reduces efficiency and is often responsible for noises.

grille: the decorative, often chrome grid on the front of an automobile through which air passes to reach the radiator

ground: an electrical strap or wire that completes an electrical circuit, returning it to the battery through the vehicle's metal frame

ground clearance: the distance from the lowest point of the vehicle (usually the differential) to the ground

halfshaft: the right-side or left-side bar or shaft between the transaxle and the wheels on a front-wheel drive vehicle

halogen headlights: modern lights with small bulbs and a bright white light (as opposed to tungsten headlights)

harmonic balancer: *see* crankshaft balancer

head gasket: the thin, flat, heat-resistant material that seals the opening where the engine block and the engine head meet

headpipes: steel exhaust pipes that carry burned combustion gases from the manifold to the catalytic converter

heads-up display: data from the instrument panel gauges that is projected onto the windshield

heater control valve: a one-way door through which coolant travels from the engine to the heater core and thus warms the car's interior

heater core: a small radiator that takes heat from hot coolant and releases it into the passenger compartment, assisted an electric fan

high intensity discharge headlight (HID): a bright long-life headlight. The bulb has been replaced by a sealed unit filled with a gas and tiny electrodes.

hood: the bodywork of the car that covers the engine; the English call it the bonnet

horsepower: a measurement of an engine's power equal to the energy needed to raise 550 pounds one foot in one second. Usually, the more horsepower an engine has, the more powerful it is.

hydraulic system: any system that operates by fluid under pressure

hydrometer: a device that measures the relative health of a battery by indicating the amount of sulfuric acid remaining in its electrolyte solution

hydroplaning: losing traction when a layer of water forms between tires and the road surface. The danger of hydroplaning is heightened with worn tires and increased speeds.

idle: describes an engine's rotational speed when the driver is not applying pressure to the gas pedal

ignition control module: a computer chip that controls the delivery of electrical current to the spark plugs by adjusting ignition timing

ignition system: the components that deliver spark to the air/fuel mixture at the correct times

independent suspension: a suspension system in which each wheel responds independently to changes in the surface of the road

input shaft: the shaft or rod leading from the engine to the transmission

insulator: material that prevents the flow of electrical current

intake manifold: metal tubing, bolted to the engine, through which the air/fuel mixture reaches the cylinders

intake port: the passageway from the intake manifold into the cylinder

intake valve: a valve through which air and fuel enter the combustion chamber

intercooler: a device used in combination with turbochargers and superchargers that cools air and adds power

intermittent wiper: adjusted by the driver, this system wipes the windshield glass at selected intervals

internal combustion: the burning of an air/fuel mixture inside an engine to produce power

jack: a hand-operated device used to raise a vehicle for servicing the underbody or changing a tire

jet: an opening through which fuel passes in a carburetor

journal: the part of a rod or shaft that turns on an engine's bearing

key fob: a small plastic control switch accompanying a remote-control locking system

knocking: a heavy metallic rattling or clicking similar to marbles or ball bearings hitting one another; often related to an irregular burning of the air/fuel mixture

lateral runout: the wobble of a tire or wheel

leaf springs: suspension components consisting of flat lengths of metal (leaves) that absorb the motion of a car's wheels

lean fuel mixture: an air/fuel mixture containing less than the correct amount of gasoline

limited slip differential: also known as positraction, this device, typically found on the rear axle of a real-wheel-drive vehicle, senses wheel spin and redirects energy to the opposite wheel

linkage: any system of rods and levers

load: the weight of an object that is being moved or the resistance of an object to being moved

load tester: a diagnostic tool that determines the health of a battery by simulating electrical loads or need

LOF: abbreviation for lube, oil, and filter; a maintenance procedure that includes lubricating a car's chassis and changing the engine oil and oil filter

lube job: a procedure to add clean grease

lubricant: any substance that protects an object by coating it with a thin film. Lubricants provide a slippery cushion that prevents friction.

lubrication system: a system for pumping oil to the working parts of an engine

lumbar support: an electrical or manual adjustment on front seats to increase back comfort

MacPherson strut: a suspension component that combines the spring and shock absorber in one unit; named after the engineer who designed it

manual transmission: a transmission in which the driver changes gears by shifting a lever; also called a standard transmission

master cylinder: a device for pressurizing fluid in hydraulic systems, usually brakes

memory seat: an adjustment feature on a power seat designed for vehicles with more than one driver. Programmable systems can remember radio, outside mirror, steering wheel, and climate control choices.

misfire: an irregularity in the igniting of the air/fuel mixture

MTBE: a synthetic gasoline additive that helps reduce pollutants.

muffler: part of the exhaust system, this device absorbs much of the sound that combustion creates by routing sound waves through hollow chambers

multi-grade oil: oil containing additives that give it the pouring qualities of more than one grade of oil

multi-port fuel injection: a computerized system that delivers an ideal amount of fuel into each cylinder through individual fuel injectors

multivalve engine: an engine equipped with additional intake and/or exhaust valves that allow for more efficient combustion

NHV: a term that refers to a vehicle's rate of noise, vibration, and harshness

octane: the rating of a gasoline's ability to resist pinging or knocking; higher numbers mean greater resistance

odometer: a dashboard instrument that records the distance that an automobile travels

oil: a liquid, usually petroleum based, that acts as a lubricant

oil filter: a pleated paper device that removes dirt and contaminants from oil

oil galley: an enclosed passageway, with smaller passageways leading from it, through which oil moves to lubricate vital engine parts

oil pressure gauge: a dashboard instrument that registers oil pressure

oil pump: a pump that circulates oil through the engine

oscilloscope: a diagnostic tool that gives a visual picture of the ignition system's activity

output shaft: the shaft leading from the transmission to the drive wheels

overdrive: also known as fifth gear; a fuel-saving cruising gear designed to be used at highway speeds

overflow reservoir: the translucent tank, part of a vehicle's cooling system, that collects expanding coolant as engine temperature's rise

overhead cam engine (OHC): a common engine layout in which the camshaft is located above the valves

oversteer: the tendency of a car to turn too sharply when cornering; results in the rear end losing traction and swinging out

oxygen sensor: a device that monitors the richness or leanness of the fuel mixture by detecting the amount of oxygen in exhaust gases

parking brake: an auxiliary brake system to hold a vehicle motionless while at rest

passive anti-theft system: a system allowing only a specially coded key to start a vehicle

pinging: a light metallic rattling or clicking similar to marbles or BBs hitting one another; often caused by faulty burning of the air/fuel mixture

piston: a cylindrical metal plug that moves up and down within a cylinder. As it moves it pulls in the air/fuel mixture, compresses it, delivers the force of the combustion explosion to the crankshaft, and expels the burned fuel. Also a device in brake systems that transmits hydraulic pressure to the brake pads.

piston ring: a metal hoop that surrounds a piston and helps prevent the escape of gases

planetary gears: gear sets that provide changes in gear ratios in automatic transmissions

play: looseness or lack of responsiveness in the steering wheel

plies: pieces of reinforcing material embedded within the rubber of a tire. The materials and the angle at which they meet each other determine the tire's construction category.

points: a component of earlier ignition systems, these metal arms open and close, initiating surges of electricity to spark plugs

port: the connecting passageway between the intake manifold and the combustion chamber

positive crankcase ventilation system: a system that picks up gases that have escaped into the crankcase from the combustion chambers and returns them to the engine to be burned

power brakes: brakes that use a pump powered by the engine to increase hydraulic pressure in the brake system

power steering: a hydraulic-powered system that makes steering easier

power train warranty: the manufacturer's guarantee that the heavier components of a vehicle, including the engine, transmission, differential, and drive axles, will be free of defects and perform in a specific way; usually longer than the bumper-to-bumber warranty

preheated air intake system: a system that warms air entering the engine to the correct temperature

pressure plate: the clutch component that squeezes the clutch disk against the flywheel when the clutch pedal is released

pretensioner: a device that automatically tightens a seat belt in an accident. It must be replaced after it has been deployed.

printed circuit: a board with a printed pattern of metal connectors that conducts current to electronic components attached to the board

PROM (programmable read-only memory): a computer chip that permanently stores information. Information on this chip cannot be changed or altered, only reviewed and read.

prorated: assessed as to compensation or value based on the proportion of the use of the item

prototype: an experimental vehicle, used to test a new design

pushrod engine: an engine in which the camshaft is placed low and operates the opening and closing of the valves through pushrods and other components

rack and pinion steering: a lightweight steering system consisting of a pinion gear (one with a small number of teeth) and a long rack with teeth

radial runout: the difference between high and low points on a tire tread

radial tire: a tire with lines (cords) that radiate symmetrically from a central point, like the spokes of a wheel. The construction materials meet each other at right angles and are reinforced with strips of steel.

radiator: a device that stores and circulates coolant to keep an engine from overheating

radiator cap: a cap that helps maintain proper pressure and temperature within the cooling system

rear integral child seat: a built-in collapsible seat with restraint straps, for children age one and older and weighing 20 to 80 pounds

rear air suspension: a computer-controlled feature that automatically adjusts as load increases to keep a vehicle level

rear-wheel drive: a drive-train layout in which power is transmitted from the engine to only the rear wheels

rebuilt: describes a part that has been restored to nearly new condition and resold as a replacement

receiver: a dryer that removes potentially destructive moisture from the air-conditioning system

refrigerant: a fluid with a low boiling point that absorbs heat; used in air-conditioning systems

relays: switches used to operate headlights, turn signals, windshield wipers, and other devices

release fork: a lever that pushes the clutch plate away from the flywheel when the clutch pedal is pushed down

resonator: a device that diminishes noise created by combustion gases as they exit the exhaust system

rich fuel mixture: an air/fuel mixture containing more than the correct amount of gasoline

ring: *see* piston ring

ring gear: the outer gear in an automatic transmission. Inside it sit the sun and planetary gears.

rocker arm: one of the components connecting the camshaft to the valves in a pushrod engine

rotor: a metal disc connected to the wheel in a braking system; an ignition component in earlier model vehicles that directs electrical current to each of the spark plugs

rotary engine: an engine that converts power directly into circular motion (unlike piston engines, which convert the up-and-down motion of pistons into circular motion)

scheduled service: preventive maintenance procedures that manufacturers recommend be performed at specific intervals

seal beam headlight: a type of headlight in which all parts are sealed in one unit

sedan: a four-door passenger car with a separate trunk, sometimes connected to the interior via a folding rear seat

seizing: when an engine's internal components are badly damaged from too much heat and abruptly stop moving; an engine meltdown

selector fork: also called a shift lever, the lever that allows the driver to select a specific gear in an automatic transmission

sending unit: a device that monitors volume or temperature

sensor: a device that receives and feeds back data

shock absorber: a sealed suspension component system filled with fluid that absorbs the impact of wheel movement on rough roads and dampens the oscillation of the coil and leaft springs

short: a fault in an electrical circuit that prevents operation of an electrical device, results in a blown fuse, or drains the battery

sludge: unburned deposits that form as a result of combustion

solar tint glass: tinted glass that protects cabin materials and passengers from the sun's more harmful, heat-producing ultraviolet rays

solenoid: an electromagnetic object that acts as a switch

spark plug: a metal and ceramic device that produces a spark

specific gravity reading: the measurement of a battery's state of charge or relative health

split-bench seat: a seat that is divided for individual comfort

spring: a suspension component that compresses and extends to absorb the motion of wheels on irregular ground

stall: the sudden stopping of an engine

starter: an electrical motor that starts the engine running by turning a crankshaft

steering: the system of rods, levers, and gears that controls the direction of a vehicle

steering gear box: a unit containing gears that changes the circular movement of the steering wheel into the side-to-side movement of the wheels

steering wheel radio/climate controls: mounted conveniently, these "redundant" controls allow hands-on driving while adjusting the radio or temperature controls

stroke: each movement of a piston, up or down

strut: a rod or bar used in the suspension system to provide structural strength

sump: the oil reservoir in the bottom of the engine block

sun gear: the central gear in an automatic transmission

supercharger: a belt-driven device that forces an engine to produce more power by breathing more air

suspension: the system—including springs, shock absorbers, and struts—that controls the car's side-to-side and up-and-down motion. The system makes for a safe and more comfortable ride.

switch: a piece of metal suspended between two pieces of wire that serves as a gate for electrical current, turning current off and on

synchronizers: toothed devices found in manual transmissions that synchronize the speeds of the gear combinations, preventing them from clashing

synthetic oil: a lubricant made in the chemist's laboratory that can reach moving parts quicker than petroleum-based oils

tachometer: an instrument that records the rotations of the crankshaft and, therefore, engine speed

tailpipe: the final exhaust pipe, through which burned gases reach the outside air

tappets: levers or cams designed to touch or tap another engine component to cause movement

thermostat: a one-way heat-sensitive door that permits the flow of coolant to the radiator once a predetermined temperature is reached

three-point lap/shoulder belts: the modern seat/shoulder belt; the primary safety device in all vehicles

throttle: a device that controls the supply of fuel

throttle body fuel injection: a mixing system that sprays a common measure of air and fuel to the cylinders

throttle position sensor: an electronic eye that relays information to the computer about the throttle opening (supply of fuel to the engine)

throw-out bearing: the doughnut-shaped bearing on which the clutch plate rests as it moves away from the flywheel and back again

tie rods: in a rack and pinion steering system, rods that connect the rack to the steering knuckle

timing belt (chain): the flexible loop of metal or reinforced rubber that drives the camshaft as the crankshaft turns

tire pressure warning system: an audible or visual warning that alerts the driver when tire pressure is lost

toe-in: a measure of front-end alignment, based on how much the front wheels point toward each other

top dead center (TDC): the uppermost point of a piston's travel within the cylinder

torque: a turning or twisting force. The torque of an engine is the maximum turning power produced at a specific speed.

torque converter: the mechanism that transfers power from the engine to the wheels in an automatic transmission

torque steer: the tendency of some front-wheel-drive vehicles to pull to one side upon acceleration

torque wrench: a specialized wrench that quantifies the amount of force applied to a bolt

torsion bar: a spring that absorbs road motion by means of a bar that twists and turns

towing capacity: a calculated industry-standard number that includes two passengers, required towing equipment, trailer and load

traction: a tire's grip on the road

traction control: usually electronically controlled, this system transfers the power of a spinning wheel to one with more grip by applying the brake to the former (or reducing engine power). Some systems are active only at low speeds; others at all speeds.

transaxle: the component that transmits the power of the engine to the front wheels in a front-wheel-drive vehicle. The transaxle combines both the transmission and the differential.

transfer case: in a four-wheel-drive vehicle, a special, third set of gears that lock the front and real wheels together, sending power to all four wheels

transmission: the gear mechanism linking the power of the engine to the wheels

transmission fluid: a lightweight oil used in an automatic transmission

transverse engine: an engine mounted so that the alignment of the cylinders is side-to-side instead of lengthwise. The engine allows for a more compact front end.

tread: the grooved face of an automobile tire

tread depth indicator: a device that is inserted into various grooves in a tire to measure tread depth

trouble code: the code number, generated by an on-board computer and stored in its memory, that specifies an engine fault or problem

trunk pass-thru: usually a small center section of the rear seat that folds down to allow unusually long items to be carried in an otherwise shallow trunk space

tune-up: the routine replacement of spark plugs, filters, and other air, fuel, and ignition-related parts, plus a precise series of tests and adjustments performed at specific intervals, for achieving maximum engine performance

tuning: adjusting the engine to regain maximum engine performance

turbine: a fanlike device with blades that spins fluids around

turbocharger: a device that uses exhaust gases to add horsepower to an engine by forcing more air into the cylinders

turning radius: a measurement of how tightly a vehicle will turn with body overhang not a factor

two-stroke engine: an engine in which combustion occurs each time the piston travels to the top of the cylinder

understeer: the tendency of a vehicle to continue going straight while cornering, despite the turning of the steering wheel

unibody: refers to a platform that uses sheet metal rather than a separate steel frame

universal joint (U-joint): the metal connecting unit that allows one end of the driveshaft to move up and down with the motion of the wheel

vacuum: negative air pressue produced by an engine and used to operate various devices

vacuum leak: the loss of vacuum in an engine as a result of a leaking gasket or hose, usually resulting in a performance problem

valve clearance: the gap between the top of the valve and the part that opens and closes it. In some vehicles, valve clearance is adjustable.

valve control body: a compartment containing tiny passageways that collect pressurized transmission fluid

valve guides: metal shells or sleeves within which valves move up and down

valves: one-way doors that regulate the flow of the air/fuel mixture into and out of the cylinders

valve seat: the surface a valve touches when it closes

valve train: components that help valves open and close, including springs, rocker arms, pushrods, and tappets

vaporize: to convert a liquid or solid substance into a gaseous one. The process may create a fine mist or spray.

vapor lock: when gasoline in the fuel lines turns from a liquid to a vapor, starving an engine of fuel

vapor storage canister: a charcoal canister that holds fuel system vapors that have been redirected from the engine for reburning

variable load shock absorber: a shock absorber that mechanically or electronically smooths the ride by responding differently to various weights carried in the car

variable ratio power steering: a power steering system in which power assistance is continually monitored and electronically adjusted for good road feel

V-belt: *see* drive belt

V-engine: an engine in which the cylinders are laid out in a V formation

ventilated disc brake: a superior disc brake with openings cut into it for quicker and more effective heat dissipation

VIN (vehicle identification number): a serial number that includes model, color, build number, date, and manufacturing location. The number is located at the base of the windshield.

viscosity: the measure of oil's ability to flow or pour at different temperatures

volatility: the ability of a substance such as gasoline to burn or explode easily

voltage: a measurement of the force or pressure of an electrical charge

voltage regulator: a device that regulates the flow of electricity from the alternator

warranty: the manufacturer's guarantee that specific components will be free of defects and perform in a specific way

wastegate: a device that regulates the amount of extra boost a turbocharger can deliver to an engine

water jacket: a system of passageways inside the engine block and head through which coolant circulates

water pump: a device that circulates coolant

wattage: the amount of power produced by an electrical current, as measured in thousands of watts or kilowatts and kilowatt-hours

wear bar: a patch of slightly raised rubber at the bottom of a tire's tread that, when visible, indicates it is time to replace the tires

wheel alignment: the adjustment or positioning of suspension components so that the car's wheels meet the road at a specific angle for longest life and best handling

wheel balancing: a procedure in which small metal weights are attached to the lighter spots on a wheel to make it turn without vibrations at higher speeds

wheelbase: the distance between the front and the rear axles

wheel bearing: a device resembling a metal doughnut with many ball bearings inside that distribute the weight and turning force of the wheel on the axle

wheel chock: a triangular piece of wood, metal, or plastic that can be placed next to a tire to keep a vehicle from rolling

wheel cylinder: a device that pushes drum brake linings outward against the brake drum, causing a wheel to slow or stop

wheel-spin: the excessive movement of a wheel that results in the loss of traction

window lock-out switch: a switch that allows a driver to override the electric switches of all passenger windows as protection for small children

wind-up: the strain felt by the power train when both axles of a standard, part-time four-wheel-drive vehicle are locked together and forced to turn at the same speed on dry pavement

winterizing: the maintenance involved in preparing a vehicle for winter

wiring harness: a group of electrical wires connecting various electrical devices

xenon headlights: superior, high-intensity lights with a blue-white light that supply maximum nighttime visibility

APPENDIX

Safety Agencies

National Highway Traffic and Safety Administration:
888/DASH-2-DOT; www.nhtsa.gov
Insurance Institute for Highway Safety: www.
highwaysafety.com

New Car and Truck Manufacturers Directory

For product information and literature:

Acura: 800/IT0-ACURA, www.honda.com

A.M. General: 800/1732-5493, www.hummer.com

Audi: 800/FOR-AUDI, www.audiusa.com

BMW: 800/334-4BMW, www.bmwusa.com

Buick: 800/4A-BUICK, www.buick.com

Cadillac: 800/333-4CAD, www.cadillac.com

Chevrolet: 800/950-2438, www.chevrolet.com

Chrysler: 800/4A-CHRYSLER, www.chryslercars.com

Dodge: 800/4A-DODGE, www.4adodge.com

Eagle: 800/2-TEST-EAGLE, www.eaglecars.com

Ferrari: 201/816-2600, www.ferrari.com

Ford: 800/258-FORD, www.ford.com

GMC: 800/GMC-TRUCK, www.gmc.com

Honda: 800/33-HONDA, www.honda.com

Hyundai: 800/826-CARS, www.hmaservice.com

Infiniti: 800/826-6500, www.infinitimotors.com

Isuzu: 800/726-2700, www.isuzu.com

Jaguar: 800/4JAGUAR, www.jaguarcars.com

Jeep: 800/925-JEEP, www.jeepunpaved.com

Kia: 800/333-4K1A, www.kia.com

Lamborghini: 904/565-9100, http://home.lamborghini.com

Land Rover: 800/FINE-4WD, http://best4x4.landrover.com

Lexus: 800/872-5398, www.lexususa.com

Lincoln: 800/446-8888, www.lincolnvehicles.com

Lotus: 800/24-LOTUS, www.lotuscars.com

Mazda: 800/639-1000, www.mazdausa.com

Mercedes-Benz: 800/FOR-MERCEDES, www.usa.
mercedesbenz.com

Mercury: 800/445-8888, www.mercuryvehicles.com

Mitsubishi: 800/555MITSU, www.mitsucars.com

Nissan: 800/NISSAN-3, www.nissanmotors.com

Oldsmobile: 800/242-OLDS, www.oldsmobile.com

Plymouth: 800/PLYMOUTH, www.plymouthcars .com

Pontiac: 800/762-4900, www.pontiac.com

Porsche: 800/PORSCHE, www.porsche.com

Rolls-Royce/Bentley: 201/967-9100

Saab: 800/SAABUSA, www.saabusa.com

Saturn: 800/522-5000, www.saturncars.com

Subaru: 800/SUBARU-3, www.subaru.com

Suzuki: 800/447-4700, www.suzukiauto.com

Toyota: 800/GO-TOYOTA: www.toyota.com

Volkswagen: 800/444-8987, www.vw.com

Volvo: 800/455-1552, www.volvocars.com

DIAGNOSTIC TOOLBOX

Following is some of the equipment professional technicians use to service your car. With these tools, the guesswork is taken out of diagnosis and service. Look for a technician or repair shop that utilizes these tools—or you may find yourself dealing with a "remove and replace" mechanic.

The test light and pressure gauge are used to determine problems with fuel pressure in the fuel delivery system.

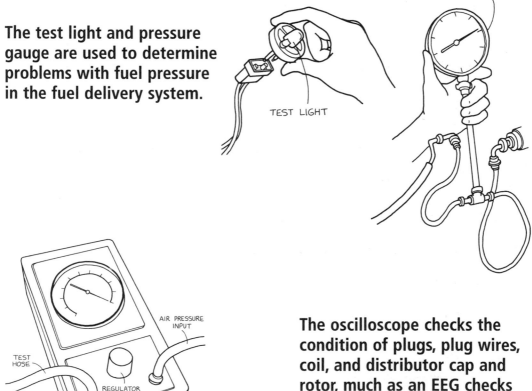

The compression tester can identify a leaky or bad head gasket, a bad valve, bad rings, and even a cracked cylinder head.

The oscilloscope checks the condition of plugs, plug wires, coil, and distributor cap and rotor, much as an EEG checks for brain waves.

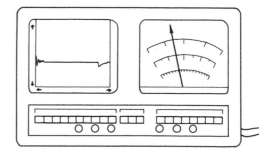

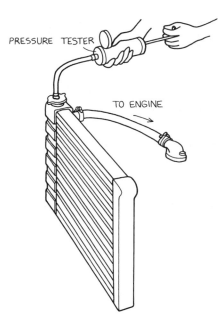

A pressure tester can pinpoint a leak in the cooling system.

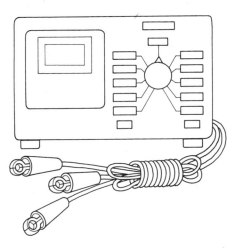

The multimeter checks the electrical system for shorts, opens, and starting problems.

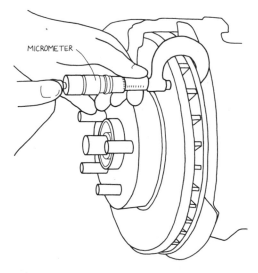

A micrometer checks the thickness of your brakes' rotors. There is a legal limit to the thickness of rotors—if yours fall below this limit, they must be replaced.

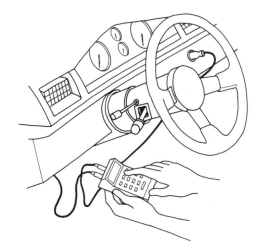

The scan tool is a device which can access the computer's trouble codes, thus identifying a multitude of problems.

TROUBLESHOOTING CHART INDEX

Following is a listing of the most common car trouble symptoms and an index to the corresponding troubleshooting chart. Identify your car's symptom and then check the troubleshooting charts on the pages listed for possible causes.

INDEX

ABOUT THE AUTHOR

Growing up as the lone girl in a family with five boys, Mary Jackson learned only the "need to know" facts about automobiles. As an adult, she began working in an auto body and repair shop, where she acquired an intense interest in automobiles.

Mary now tours the United States and Canada conducting car-care workshops and promoting "automobile literacy." She has written for newspapers and magazines, spoken on radio and television, and hosted video productions for automobile manufacturers.

Mary is a member of the Automotive Journalists Association. She lives near Boulder, Colorado, with her husband, Jim, and dog, Max.